Cambridge Elements

Elements in Islam and the Sciences
edited by
Nidhal Guessoum
American University of Sharjah, United Arab Emirates
Stefano Bigliardi
Al Akhawayn University in Ifrane, Morocco

ISLAM AND ENVIRONMENTAL ETHICS

Muhammad Yaseen Gada
Central University of Kashmir

CAMBRIDGE
UNIVERSITY PRESS

CAMBRIDGE
UNIVERSITY PRESS

Shaftesbury Road, Cambridge CB2 8EA, United Kingdom

One Liberty Plaza, 20th Floor, New York, NY 10006, USA

477 Williamstown Road, Port Melbourne, VIC 3207, Australia

314–321, 3rd Floor, Plot 3, Splendor Forum, Jasola District Centre, New Delhi – 110025, India

103 Penang Road, #05–06/07, Visioncrest Commercial, Singapore 238467

Cambridge University Press is part of Cambridge University Press & Assessment, a department of the University of Cambridge.

We share the University's mission to contribute to society through the pursuit of education, learning and research at the highest international levels of excellence.

www.cambridge.org
Information on this title: www.cambridge.org/9781009494557

DOI: 10.1017/9781009308236

When citing this work, please include a reference to the DOI 10.1017/9781009308236

First published 2024

A catalogue record for this publication is available from the British Library.

ISBN 978-1-009-49455-7 Hardback
ISBN 978-1-009-30824-3 Paperback
ISSN 2754-7094 (online)
ISSN 2754-7086 (print)

Islam and Environmental Ethics

Elements in Islam and the Sciences

DOI: 10.1017/9781009308236
First published online: April 2024

Muhammad Yaseen Gada
Central University of Kashmir

Author for correspondence: Muhammad Yaseen Gada,
myyaseenm2@gmail.com

Abstract: This Element explores environmental ethics in Islam. Its core argument is that Islamic culture and civilization are rich in environmental concerns; Islam has unique considerations and directions about what sort of human–nature relationship there should be. Muslim environmental commentators have explored basic environmental or eco-ethical principles that are deeply embedded in the Qur'an and Sunnah. Protecting and conserving the environment are not only moral duties but also an obligation in Islam. The Islamic environmental ethical system offers both conceptual paradigms and operational components to realize environmental justice and sustainable development.

Keywords: Islam, environment, ethics, Tawhid, nature

ISBNs: 9781009494557 (HB), 9781009308243 (PB), 9781009308236 (OC)
ISSNs: 2754-7094 (online), 2754-7086 (print)

Contents

Introduction

This Element is organized into six sections, along with an Introduction and a Conclusion.

Section 1 delves into the ongoing global environmental crisis. It analyzes how these problems have emerged as a result of the modern consumerist outlook and uncontrolled economic pursuits that disregard essential human values and responsibilities toward nature and fellow human beings.

Section 2 begins by elucidating the concept and significance of ethics; then it moves on to exploring modern approaches to environmental ethics through seven predominant philosophical perspectives: anthropocentrism, biocentrism, sentiocentrism, ecocentrism, deep ecology, ecofeminism, and social ecology. This section ends with some thoughts about the necessity of a theocentric approach, whose Islamic version will be explored in Sections 4 and 5.

Section 3 looks at classical Islamic works that contain abundant references to nature as well as at nature-related practices and jurisprudence that were developed in premodern times.

Section 4, after an introduction to the three main approaches to Islamic eco-theology adopted in the contemporary debate, offers an overview of the positions advanced by notable authors.

Section 5 forms the major portion of this Element. After a discussion of the distinctive features of Islamic theocentrism as well as of the references to nature in the scriptures of Islam, it explores fundamental environmental ethical principles derived from Islamic sources: "unity" (*tawḥīd*), "stewardship" (*khilāfah*), "trusteeship" (*amānah*) and accountability (*ākhirah*), "balance" (*mīzān*), and "natural disposition" (*fiṭrah*). Additionally, the section offers Islamic environmental guidelines that promote moderation, the avoidance of waste and corruption, the preservation of the Earth's beauty and cleanliness, the recognition of the rights of animals and plants, and the significance of, and respect for, water.

Section 6 highlights various initiatives taken by Muslims today to combat escalating environmental degradation through the lens of the "ecotheological" paradigm. Case studies from Zanzibar, Indonesia, Qatar, Egypt, Africa, the UK, and the US illustrate how Islamic ethics have been harnessed in diverse forms to inspire positive behavioral changes among Muslims toward nature. The section briefly touches upon the interfaith approach as well.

In the Conclusion section, I summarize the key findings of the study and I provide recommendations as practical guidelines to tackle the present environmental crisis and foster sustainable practices.

1 Current Environmental Problems

A universally acknowledged axiom asserts the vital importance of the environment for the existence of any organism. All organisms, including humans, rely on their environment and engage in ongoing interactions with their surroundings, which encompass both the nonliving (abiotic) and living (biotic) domains. However, these spheres continuously struggle with each other for survival. Over time, organisms have evolved and developed strategies to combat threats, though with limitations. As a result, certain significant changes in the environment can present formidable challenges to the survival of organisms. Natural disasters such as floods, fires, or volcanic eruptions are some of the most notable changes that are disastrous to our environment.

While natural processes are beneficial to the environment, natural disasters can cause significant damage to ecosystems, biodiversity, and the environment as a whole (Nelson, 2018; Cleveland Museum of Natural History, 2020). Can these be termed "environmental problems"? Of course, yes, natural disasters are often seen as acts of nature, this may be true for natural hazards, but their classification depends on human impacts, like loss of life or property damage. Over the past many years, mounting evidence suggests that human activities may be causing an increase in certain disasters, like floods (Guha-Sapir, 2004, p. 14). Thus, an environmental problem is characterized as any change in the physical environment's condition arising from human involvement in the environment (Glasbergen & Blowers, 1995, p. 32).

1.1 Glimpses of the Current Environmental Crisis

In the twenty-first century, human beings face unprecedented environmental challenges. This is mainly due to increasing human activity, which has put our survival at stake. The primary three unprecedented yet mutually overlapping challenges are "climate change, biodiversity loss, and overuse of critical natural resources" (Lundburg, 2019).

The Earth's climate change has had a significant detrimental impact on biodiversity, leading to notable instances of mass extinctions (Desjardins, 2013, p. xi). It has changed the way things work in our oceans, lands, and freshwater areas everywhere in the world. This has caused some local animals and plants to disappear, made diseases more common, and led to many plants and animals dying in large numbers. The human population is growing at an exponential rate. Air, water, and soil, the natural resources that sustain life on the Earth, are being exhausted or polluted at alarming rates. Toxic waste that will affect future generations continues to amass on a global scale. Similarly, forests, grasslands, wetlands, and mountains are being overgrazed and developed. Environmental data reveal the harm we have caused to the Earth. The following information presents a gloomy picture of our planet.

Environmental pollution growth is alarming and could lead to an irreversible change.

(a) Air pollution kills about seven million people every year: According to a WHO report, "[e]very year, exposure to air pollution is estimated to cause seven million premature deaths and result in the loss of millions more healthy years of life" (WHO, 2021). The report further emphasized that air pollution is one of the biggest environmental problems threatening human survival.

(b) Land-based sources account for 80 percent of marine pollution: Against the backdrop of the Rio+20 International Conference on Sustainable Development (2012), aimed at reconciling economic and environmental goals, it was observed that globally "Land-based sources account for approximately 80 percent of marine pollution" (UNESCO, 2012, p. 5). Plastic pollution, along with other causes such as industrial and agricultural wastes, coastal development, overfishing, illegal fishing, and Greenhouse Gas emissions, is responsible for the mass extinction of marine species and health problems for marine life and human beings.

(c) Close to 1.6 billion people globally do not have access to clean water: In 2020, "1 in 4 people globally do not have access to safe drinking water" (WHO & UNICEF, 2021). Millions of lives are lost annually due to contaminated water and poor hygiene and sanitation, especially in developing countries.

(d) We lose around ten million hectares of forest every single year: It is estimated that, on average, we lost nearly 8.3 million acres of tropical forests a year from 2002 to 2019, which is larger than the area of Belgium in a year (Weisse & Goldman, 2020).

(e) There has been a growth of 1.1 percent in global greenhouse gas emissions in 2019: The exponential growth in global greenhouse gas emissions disrupts the Earth's temperature, which leads to global warming and other associated environmental problems. A significant share of these greenhouse gases comes from CO_2 emissions, which consist of 74 percent, followed by other significant shares from methane, nitrous oxide, and fluorinated gases with 17 percent, 5 percent, and 3 percent, respectively (Olivier & Peters, 2020, p. 4).

Humans are the number one cause of environmental degradation, pollution, and exploitation. These statistical data clearly show that human activities, particularly in the postindustrial revolution period, driven by a materialistic outlook, have severely impacted our environment, including land, water, and air.

1.2 Global Problems of Consumer Culture

Every day, new advancements in material production and success are recorded and celebrated in the name of "modernity" and "discovery," even though some/many of these achievements will undoubtedly have an irreversible impact on our environment. The modern lifestyle that is driven by the unending pursuit of material wealth, possessions, and worldly success has taught humans to be in a race to win, regardless of the objectives and consequences. This hysteria all over the world though it thrills for the time being, it presents an alarming picture of our consumerist viewpoint. This section shows how our consumer preferences, behavioral choices, and materialist outlook affect our environment and survival.

Humans' behavior, lifestyle, practices, tastes, and policies connect them to environmental issues. This is predominantly the case with consumption patterns and longings. The following examples show the extent of consumerism's contribution to the burden and exploitation of the environment.

(a) Global Energy Consumption: World energy consumption has shown an increase of 5 percent in 2021 (TEC, 2022). The industrial and energy sectors are typically the largest sources of carbon dioxide (CO_2) emissions into the atmosphere (C2ES, 2023). Approximately 25 percent of such energy consumption is used in the automobile industry (Rodrigue, 2020, p. 124).

(b) Two new cars hit the road every second: The world produced 79.1 million automobiles in 2021, an increase of 1.3 percent compared to 2020 (ACEA, 2022).

(c) The fast fashion industry produces more carbon than international flights and maritime shipping (WB, 2019): Fast fashion refers to the production and promotion of cheap, readily disposable, yet fashionable garments (Anguelov, 2016, p. 3), and it is now a significant source of global carbon emissions, contributing almost 10 percent to the world's total emission. The fashion consumption market surged by 60 percent from 2000 to 2014, putting immense pressure on the environment. The industry's environmental impact stems from its large-scale production, short product lifecycles, extensive global supply chains, and heavy use of synthetic fibers. Unfortunately, the shift in lifestyle choices favors buying new clothes over sustainable actions like recycling and reuse, worsening the environmental consequences due to increased production.

1.3 Impact of Modern Science and Technology on the Environment

Science and technology have been generally seen as offering solutions to practical problems. No doubt, they have brought substantial changes to our lives. The things that were only dreamt of in the preindustrial era are now readily available at the touch of a finger. Today we are entangled with technology. Some scholars argue that "we are inherently technological beings and that the biological evolution that made us human was inextricably bound with the evolution of our early technology. . . . Technology has been with us as long as we have been human, and any concept of humans without technology is meaningless" (Degregori, 2002, p. xiii). However, the unrestricted use of technology for material pursuit raises serious concerns about what Obeidat (2022) sees as modernity's negative environmental impact. Environmental concerns about modern technologies such as nanotechnology, reengineering, and genetic engineering are still relatively unknown (Watt, 1988, p. 307; Stander, 2011, p. 470).

1.4 Military, War, and Weapons of Mass Destruction (WMD)

Today, humans are equipped with highly sophisticated arms and weapons (chemical and nuclear), which pose a potential threat to their survival. Modern science has created uniquely powerful and destructive military technologies and weapons. Weapons of mass destruction (WMD) come in various sizes, types, and yields, such as nuclear, chemical, biological, and the missile technology. These have put human rights, especially the environmental rights of poor, defenseless people, in danger. What is more surprising and unfortunate is that the ecological destruction brought about by these weapons is often considered a result of military exercises, such as weapon testing and combat practice, often leading to substantial ecological destruction (Thanikodi & Kanagaraj, 2009; Smith, 2017; London & White, 2019). The worst type of weapon is the nuclear weapon, which can cause enormous death and destruction to humans and the environment. Intense heat and radiation produced by a nuclear attack will have a severe effect on the geosphere, the atmosphere, and the biosphere (Westing, 1981, p. 272). Even as the immediate impacts on lives, health, buildings, public facilities, and the means of production die down, "nuclear explosions might drastically alter if not perhaps fatally impair the life support systems of the globe" (London & White, 2019, p. 2), and studies indicate that ill effects could persist for years. Humanity has already witnessed the crippling effects of nuclear weapons on humans and the environment.

1.5 Water Disputes

Water is essential to human survival and a basic requirement of life. Though abundant, freshwater is limited (which is only 2.5 percent, of which two-thirds are locked in the glaciers and ice caps), and worldwide demand for freshwater is rising exponentially due to large-scale urbanization across the globe. In addition, environmental degradation and climate change seriously affect seasonal and regional water availability and quality. Scientists and policymakers agree that a global freshwater crisis is underway. The magnitude and content of this crisis vary greatly across areas, subregions, and countries, and its causes and reversibility are hotly debated. The crisis' existence, however, is no longer disputed. In contrast, its enormous scope, potentially catastrophic implications, and impending threats to the political stability and security of the world's numerous water crisis-affected countries are now frequent concerns in scholarly literature and worldwide public discourse (Westing, 1986; Wirsing *et al.*, 2013, p. 3).

The current international water conflicts occur mainly in the Middle East (disputes over Euphrates and Tigris Rivers among Turkey, Syria, and Iraq; and the Jordan River conflict among Israel, Lebanon, Jordan, and the State of Palestine), Africa (Nile River conflicts among Egypt, Sudan, and Ethiopia), Central Asia (the Aral Sea conflict among Kazakhstan, Uzbekistan, Turkmenistan, Tajikistan, and Kyrgyzstan), South Asia (Indus River conflict between India and Pakistan), North America (Colorado River conflict between US and Mexico), and so on (see, e.g., Just & Netanyahu, 1998; Kameri-Mbote, 2007; Everard, 2013; Wirsing, *et al.*, 2013). Though many conferences, bilateral agreements, and cooperation were accomplished to resolve water conflicts and crises, no significant change is observable on the ground.

1.6 Apathy toward Environment in Non-Muslim Countries and Other International Bodies

There is a consensus among world leaders and policymakers that immediate action is imperative to save the planet from the worst climatic impacts. Over the last thirty years, world leaders and diplomats have been formulating a framework for action to stop human-made climate change. In June 1992, 154 parties signed an international environmental treaty, the United Nations Framework Convention on Climate Change, to adopt environment-friendly policies. However, the parties disagreed on measures to limit emissions of greenhouse gases. Five years later, the parties gathered in 1997 for COP3 in Kyoto (Japan), to complete the framework when diplomats adopted the "Kyoto Protocol," which sets targets and deadlines for thirty-eight industrialized-country parties to cut their collective emissions of six GHGs (CO_2, methane, HFCs, nitrous oxide, perfluorocarbons, and sulphur hexafluoride). The US, which had backed equal reductions for all developed countries, advocated the concept of differentiation to meet the economic burden that affects some states with equal emission reductions. The US delegation said it could not accept emissions unless major developing countries also agreed to binding emission reductions, a condition demanded by the US Senate. This proposal was rejected by China, India, and other developing countries; rather, they endorsed the principle of "common but differentiated responsibilities" (CBDR) (Chasek, 2018, pp. 170–171). Since the problem was seen as "the tragedy of the commons" (Conca, 2019, p. 19) and given the individual countries' differential potentials and economic concerns, responsibilities were mainly put on developed/industrialized countries with financial obligations because these were seen as the biggest emitters of greenhouse gases.

Similarly, in December 2015, the Paris Agreement was adopted by 196 parties of the UNFCC. The Paris agreement replaced the 1997 Kyoto Protocol, which expired in 2020. The Kyoto Protocol consisted of multiple commitment periods. The initial one spanned from 2008 to 2012, followed by the agreement on a second commitment period, known as the Doha Amendment, in 2012 lasting until 2020. However, the Doha Amendment did not become effective until 2020. The international agreements on limiting climate change have advanced well (see Sachs, *et al.*, 2022), but the ratification and implementation of them remain uncertain, rather than being well respected by major developed countries. The US, Canada, Japan, Russia, and New Zealand either pulled out of or did not ratify the Kyoto Protocol because their economic interests were hurt by limiting CO_2 emissions.

The lack of commitment to uphold various international climate agreements raises concerns about the dedication of developed countries toward addressing climate change. Scholarly literature and policymakers are increasingly concerned about the ethical systems and sensitivity of our responsibilities to people who are directly or indirectly affected by our actions (see McKibben, 1999; Brown, 2001). The costs of apathy and a lack of commitment to climate change are far higher. Ultimately, it is all about the free market economy; the pursuit of profit, guided by market forces, tends to prioritize short-term gains and overlook the long-term environmental consequences of economic activities. Consequently, within this economic framework, individuals may find limited incentives or opportunities to actively engage with or prioritize environmental concerns.

1.7 Muslim Apathy toward Environment

Globally, Islam is the world's second-largest religion, with 1.9 billion adherents, as projected by Pew Research (2011), constituting about 24.9 percent of the world's population. There are fifty Muslim-majority countries worldwide, with a majority falling in the MENA (Middle East and North Africa) region. However, the MENA region only represents about 20 percent of the total Muslim population, and more than 60 percent of Muslims are concentrated in Asia, with Indonesia as the most prominent Muslim populous country (12.6 percent), followed by the Indian Muslim minority (11.1 percent) (Pew Research Centre, 2019).

Muslims comprise a disproportionate share of the world's poor, who are vulnerable to and suffer significantly from the impacts of environmental degradation, such as climate change and water shortages. However, like governments in other non-Muslim countries, governments in Muslim societies have been slow to respond to environmental issues, even though most Muslims regard environmental degradation, including climate change, as a serious problem. This disparity in interest or limited engagement toward taking action can be attributed, in part, to the economic challenges – debt burden, trade barriers, economic dependence, structural adjustment programs, resource exploitation, lack of technological transfer, climate change responsibility – imposed by industrialized nations on developing countries.

The economic challenge to Muslim-majority countries is especially worrisome, which is reflected in the prioritization of economic growth and poverty alleviation over climate change mitigation (Koehrsen, 2021, p. 3; Abed & Davoodi, 2003). Based on diverse geography, ecology, availability of natural resources, and economic development, the economies of the MENA region depend largely on the available natural resources, which means more burdens on the environment, and hence rendering the region particularly susceptible to challenges like freshwater crises and escalating heat waves. Furthermore, the adverse consequences of overextracting oil resources compound these environmental issues, exacerbating the overall situation faced by the MENA region. Equally important is the unprecedented urbanization and overdependence on technology at the cost of catastrophic climate change. On the other hand, Asian-Pacific Muslim countries, such as Indonesia, Bangladesh, Pakistan, and others, have faced adverse weather conditions like frequent floods, droughts, heavy rainfall, soil erosion, and sea level rise. Perhaps, deforestation is the single most important cause of radical climate change in the Muslim countries of the Asia-Pacific region.

Muslim perspectives differ on how environmental crises emerge and who is to blame. In addition, Muslims' general apathy for environmental degradation is also attributed to how they interpret climate change. Based on different interpretations, Muslim responses to environmental crises have generated different approaches (discussed in Section 4). According to Koehrsen (2021, p. 3), generally, the interpretations of climate change are summarized into three types: (a) climate change by human-induced actions; (b) spiritual crisis; and (c) Western intervention in the Muslim world. The categories are not mutually exclusive.

2 Environmental Ethics and Contested Frameworks

2.1 The Meaning of Ethics

The word "ethics" comes from the Greek word *ethos*, meaning "habit," "custom," "usage," or "manners" (Zaroug, 1999, p. 46; Tiles, 2000, p. 3). Ethics can be regarded as the study and practice of moral behaviour shaped by societal norms, customs, and habitual patterns of conduct. Generally, however, the term refers to principles and values related to right and wrong conduct or behaviour; according to such a meaning, ethics can be defined as "rules for behavior in accordance with a system of values" (Gillette, 2005, p. 301). In a broader perspective, ethics is the study of right conduct: What we ought to do, how we ought to live, what type of people we should be, and what sort of society we should have, are all examples of ethical questions.

Extending ethics to the natural environment has been a general concern of many ethicists, environmentalists, and other scholars. Environmental ethics deals, as Yang (2006), a noted environmentalist, says, "with the ethical problems surrounding environmental protection, and it aims to provide ethical justification and moral motivation for the issue of global environmental protection." In a similar vein, Brennan (2002) defines environmental ethics as "the discipline that studies the moral relationship of human beings to, and also the value and moral status of, the environment and its nonhuman contents."

2.2 Why Environmental Ethics? Setting the Background

Owing to the pressing and ubiquitous environmental problems, environmentalists were perplexed with the question of whether a new approach to ethics is required to solve the environmental crisis. It is true that environmental ethics has been criticized for being unfeasible and unnecessary in the presence of the already existing discipline of traditional ethics (or interpersonal ethics) (Dickson, 2000; Attfield, 2003; Kawall, 2017). However, scholarly literature identifies environmental ethics as having tremendous potential to mitigate the environmental crisis.

Traditional ethical theory primarily focuses on the relationship between individual fellow humans and behaviors toward and between groups of humans. Moreover, environmental issues also raise multiple social issues such as social justice or unequal exposure to pollution and access to natural resources. Hence, critics often overlook distinguishing between environmental and traditional ethics, which are intertwined and mutually reinforcing, to the extent that it becomes difficult to draw a demarcation between them.

Environmental specialists assert that environmental ethics has some distinctive features – extended, interdisciplinary, plural, global, and revolutionary – that make it different from traditional ethical theory. First, it is a relatively new field, and a comparatively underdeveloped one, in which the human–nature relationship is predominant. Furthermore, crucial environmental issues such as climate change, water shortage, biodiversity loss, and food security raise specific value questions. In addition, the importance of environmental considerations continues to be overlooked in comparison to traditional ethics, despite the rise in environmental consciousness and awareness over the past few decades (Routley, 1973; Hens, 1998; Yang, 2006; Jamieson, 2008, p. 69; Sandler, 2018, pp. 7–8;). Environmental ethicists, thus, are exploring new approaches to establishing environmental ethics.

From the beginnings of environmental literature in the 1960s and 1970s, a few key questions have made people think about whether nature has any value on its own. In any ethical theory, two questions are of considerable importance: "What kinds of things are intrinsically valuable, good or bad?" and "What makes an action right or wrong?" (Singer, 1999, p. 148; Brennan, 2002; Jamieson, 2008, pp. 67–68; Attfield, 2016; Droz, 2022).

Addressing the first question, "value theory" discusses the distinction between *intrinsic value* (inherent value) and *instrumental value*. Such a theory underlines the question of assigning "what type of value to what entities"; it is also of crucial importance in environmental ethics (Palmer, 2012, p. 12; Droz, 2022, p. 7). Something has intrinsic worth if it is inherently good, desirable, or of ultimate value *in itself*.

In contrast, something of "instrumental value" is valuable only as a means to the realization of some other purpose or an end other than *itself*. Many scholars attempt to explain the concept of "value" by using examples; for instance, they point out that pleasure has intrinsic value in itself because most of us desire it for its own sake. Money has merely instrumental value because we desire it to buy our material needs. However, we would not want money if we were stranded on a desert island. On the other hand, happiness is just as important to us no matter where we are (see, e.g., Singer, 1999, p. 148; Jamieson, 2008, pp. 69–70). An equally important concern is what makes an action "good" or "bad"; this poses great challenges to many ethical theorists as it entails ontological and epistemological bases.

2.3 Contested Frameworks in Environmental Ethics

Modern specialists and environmental ethicists have devised considerably different approaches and theories to address these difficult questions. These theories have different implications for how we approach environmental problems. In the West, "environmental ethics" refers to a wide spectrum of perspectives ranging from extreme anthropocentrism to simple biocentrism to the most radical ecocentrism.

2.3.1 Anthropocentrism

Anthropocentrism, literally "human-centered," is a value theory or ethical viewpoint that holds that all and only human beings, their lives and experiences, have intrinsic (or inherent) value or are morally significant. Consequently, everything in the nonhuman world, such as animals, plants, other living organisms, complex ecosystems, and the natural world, possess only instrumental value relative to human beings for their benefit and welfare. The nonhuman world has no moral significance or standing of its own; therefore, they have no moral consideration. As a result, there is no ethical implication in the human–nature relationship. In this viewpoint, environmental protection or degradation matters only insofar as it affects human interests alone (Robinson, 2002, p. 113; Yang, 2006; p. 28; Thompson, 2017, p. 77; Tucker & John, 2017, pp. 4–5).

Many environmental ethicists, however, consider anthropocentrism the ideological source, not the solution, of our environmental crisis. The underlying ideology fostered the notion that humans were distinct from nature, thereby asserting their authority to use it for the benefit of human well-being. This individualistic or humanistic worldview led Lynn White Jr. (1967), a prominent American historian, to write an influential article titled "The Historical Roots of Our Ecological Crisis." In the article, White explains the philosophical and intellectual roots of the ecological crisis, specifically blaming Christianity for it.

This was not the first scholarly concern in response to the mounting environmental crisis; earlier in the 1960s, a series of notable and influential publications and newspaper articles, apart from radio programs, galvanized environmental consciousness in the public mind and helped change environmental attitudes. For example, Rachel Carson's (1963) book *Silent Spring* stands out for its combination of precise analysis and broad insights on the detrimental health impacts of the overuse of pesticides and insecticides in the agricultural industry on humans and ecosystems. A well-trained scientist, Carson, however, was criticized by industry and government representatives; she was accused of being "hysterically overemphatic" with a "mystical attachment to the balance of nature" (Gershon, 2019).

The impact of White's arguments on environmentalists, philosophers, thinkers, religious scholars, and policymakers concerned with the environmental crisis was immediate and far-reaching. His key concerns were discussed and looked upon in a wide range of environmental literature (see, Spencer, 2019). Though he also received criticism, particularly for making the Christian religion responsible for current environmental problems, White's discourse initiated a series of arguments and counterarguments that considerably enriched environmental ethical theories and approaches. In particular, it led to the development of nonanthropocentrism, a new viewpoint with varied interpretations and implications; it also stimulated many scholars to refine and reinterpret the anthropocentric view.

Other notable contributions from the 1960s include Paul Erlich's (1968) book *The Population Bomb* and Garrett Hardin's (1968) article "The Tragedy of the Commons"; both warn about the perils of overpopulation, including environmental deterioration, mass starvation, and societal upheaval. These scholarly writings were widely read, enjoyed, and discussed in academia and the media. Thus, the environmental debates, which were earlier considered "to be against modernity, economic progress, and against the 'holy' development itself" during the environmental movements of the 1960s and 1970s, were no longer a controversial topic in the 1990s (Ouis, 2003).

Environmentalists began to distinguish and carve out *transgenerational* anthropocentrism from *traditional* anthropocentrism. In sum, the former encourages to care for both present and future human generations while using the natural environment (Stenmark, 2009, p. 83). Redefining and defending anthropocentrism, Bryan Norton (1984) further distinguishes between *reasoned* and *felt* preferences, where every preference or action is not morally justified; rather, a particular reasoned preference is morally justified and acceptable only when it is critically examined according to a reasonable worldview (Norton, 1984, p. 134; Yang, 2006). However, other *transgenerational* anthropocentric ethicists acknowledge that nature possesses some intrinsic (or inherent) moral worth. This polarization over intrinsic value between humans and nonhumans resulted in other environmental viewpoints, which broadly oscillate between anthropocentric and nonanthropocentric positions.

Nonanthropocentrism is an ethical perspective on nonhuman natural beings who have intrinsic or inherent value and are thus morally distinct from humans. Nonanthopocentrists argue that moral value cannot be determined or justified solely in terms of human interests and, as a result, propose several alternative moral value bases. Thus, depending on whether all extra-human entities have any intrinsic value or are restricted to some rational beings, nonanthropocentrism can be broadly categorized into three ethical value theories: biocentrism, sentiocentrism, and ecocentrism.

2.3.2 Biocentrism

Literally meaning *life-centered*, biocentrism is broadly defined as an ethical viewpoint that maintains that all individual living forms have intrinsic worth. Consequently, individual living creatures, based on their biological characteristics, have moral standing, and deserve respect and moral consideration for what they are (Robinson, 2002; Stenmark, 2009, p. 83; Yang, 2006; Thomson, 2017, p. 80; Attfield, 2018). In this case, the human–nature relationship is evaluated based on how it affects only living beings, including humans. Moreover, theorists argue that living organisms' interests are morally relevant whether they are conscious of them or not. Hence, in biocentrism, at least, some living forms apart from humans have intrinsic worth or moral standing, but since ecosystems or other species are not living forms per se, they lack inherent worth or moral consideration – an assumption, however, that ecocentrists reject.

Advocates of biocentrism, generally, believe that all living individuals have equal intrinsic worth because they are as good as humans are. Thus, all living organisms deserve equal respect because they possess equal moral status. This is an example of holistic biocentrism, which confers intrinsic value on collectives rather than individual members of a species.

The critics of biocentrism nevertheless respond by arguing that biocentrism, in general, confers equal inherent moral worth and standing to all living organisms, from a small fly to a human being (Callicott, 2017, p. 364). This perspective introduces a different worldview that supports the idea of granting moral consideration exclusively to conscious beings, including all living animals.

2.3.3 Sentiocentrism

Sentiocentrism, or animal-centeredness, is a value theory in environmental ethics that holds that all animals, at least those who are sentient, have inherent moral value. Thus, humans have a duty to respect the rights and interests of animals. The underlying philosophy of sentiocentrism considers animals' experiences of suffering and cruelty to warrant direct moral consideration. Animal liberationists such as Singer (1975) and Regan (1979, 1980) contend that animals can perceive pain and pleasure; thus, their sentience is a sufficient and necessary reason to accord them moral status. Hence, the appropriate way to treat animals is to consider them as ends in themselves and not as means to satisfy human interests (Taylor, 1986, p. 155).

Animal ethicists contest anthropocentric viewpoint which entitles human beings to exclusive moral worth. Human beings are treated as superior just on the basis of being rational entities, and humans are seen as the builders of human civilization. Several nonanthropocentric theorists endorse criticism against the human-centric worldview – a view termed as "human chauvinism," "arbitrary discrimination," "morally unjustified," "biased determination," and so on (Thompson, 2017, pp. 83–84). Others maintain that some humans are, in fact, rational and thus moral agents capable of reciprocal concerns and being able to make decisions, not all are. On the other hand, some animals are more capable than some humans of doing these things. Certain animals, specifically octopuses and orangutans, exhibit a higher degree of self-consciousness compared to some humans who struggle with, or lack, the capacity for effective cooperation and social organization. Similarly, Ronald Sandler, author and professor of philosophy, writes that "some nonhuman animals have equal or greater psychological capacities than do some human beings, and so have comparable or even more complex and diverse interests" (Sandler, 2018, p. 99). As a result of Sandler's recognition of comparable psychological capacities in some nonhuman animals, J. Baird Callicott (b. 1941), American philosopher and scholar, asserts that the fundamental characteristic that grants intrinsic value and justifies ethical consideration is the status of being a "subject of a life," capable of experiencing favorable and unfavorable circumstances from its own perspective (Callicott, 2017, p. 367). "Subject of a life" means having the ability to have preferences, desires, sensations, and feelings that contribute to one's overall well-being or suffering. Essentially, it signifies having a subjective perspective on life, wherein one can perceive their own experiences as either positive or negative. This perspective, according to Callicott, conveniently extends value, ethical considerations, and rights to nonhuman animals.

However, environmental ethicists and some philosophers register strong objections against both biocentrism and sentiocentrism, contending that such positions fail to engage with the moral worth of ecology. Unable to provide a new paradigm shift acknowledging ecological insights, biocentrism and sentiocentrism overlook the moral worth of nature itself. The challenge lies in extending moral principles to nonhuman entities without fully acknowledging the value of all animal life, creating an idealistic scenario where every living form is presumed to have rights against each other, exposing a flaw in this value theory. Hence, the ideal situation involves adopting a new moral system that recognizes the moral importance of entire ecosystems. This is what is referred to as the "ecocentric paradigm."

2.3.4 Ecocentrism

Ecocentrism, or "land ethic," a nonanthropocentric ethical view, maintains that nature as a whole has intrinsic value regardless of whether it has instrumental value to humans or not. Land ethicists expand value ethic theory to include the diversity of nonhuman entities: species, ecosystems, land, soil, air, water, mountains, resources, and so on. Hence, in this case, the human–nature relationship is evaluated based on how far it affects the natural environment, including species and ecosystems. This viewpoint was originally advanced by Aldo Leopold (1887–1958), an American forester, wildlife biologist, and environmentalist.

As an ecocentrist, Leopold is known for his "Land Ethic" or "Leopoldian Land Ethic," according to which respect is due to nature as a whole and not to individual living beings. This philosophical view identifies a change of role for the human being: from "conqueror of the land community to plain member and citizen of it"; this implies, for the human being, "respect for his fellow members, as well as respect for the community as such" (Leopold, 1949, p. 204). Like White (1967), Leopold was also critical of the Judeo-Christian tradition. He writes: "Conservation is getting nowhere because it is incompatible with our Abrahamic [i.e., biblical] concept of land. We abuse land because we regard it as a commodity that belongs to us" (Leopold, 1949, p. viii). This led him to formulate his famous maxim: "A thing is right when it tends to preserve the integrity, stability, and beauty of the biotic community. It is wrong when it tends otherwise" (p. 224).

Leopold's land ethic reflects an "egalitarian" social model of nature in which humans are only "plain members and citizens" of the "biotic community." It views nature as a cohesive societal entity, emphasizing the interconnectedness and interdependence of its various components. While all ecocentrists attach a value premium to ecological diversity, ecocentrists disagree on how to best address today's environmental challenges. Nevertheless, also this outlook comes under criticism; some view ecocentrism as "environmental fascism" (Jamieson, 2008, p. 152). It is often seen as a frustrated response to sentiocentrism and biocentrists' concerns about moral extensionism. Some critics claim that Leopold's land ethic would suggest that it is more morally permissible to kill a human than an endangered wildflower, as biotic concerns and interests precede individual rights; or, to put it differently, according to some critics ecocentrism implies that the value of a human being is no longer more significant than any other component of biotic or abiotic communities (see Nash, 1989, p. 153; Hiller, 2017, p. 202). This may explain why ecocentrism is not a widely embraced perspective.

Ultimately, different ethical value theories – anthropocentrism, biocentrism, sentiocentrism, and ecocentrism – disagree on whether extra-human natural things have intrinsic value. As such, environmentalist ethicists debate whether animals, plants, species, ecosystems, and so on should be attributed equal moral worth or receive equivalent moral consideration.

2.3.5 Deep Ecology

Deep ecology is an environmental philosophy and social movement, which asserts that humans are interconnected with the entire web of life. It promotes an inherent value of all life forms and ecosystems, arguing that they have a right to exist and flourish independent of their utility to humans. Arne Naess (1912–2009), a Norwegian philosopher, is renowned for his contributions to deep ecology movement that has had a lasting impact on the discourse surrounding environmental ethics and sustainability. Naess fundamentally challenges anthropocentric perspectives on nature and advocates for a more holistic and ecocentric worldview. His philosophy, first articulated in the 1973 essay "The Shallow and the Deep, Long-Range Ecology Movement," posits that traditional environmentalism, often characterized as "shallow ecology," is insufficient in addressing the ecological crises facing the planet. Shallow ecology tends to focus on the preservation of the environment primarily for human benefit, ignoring the intrinsic value of nonhuman life forms and ecosystems.

One of Naess' key concepts is the notion of the "ecological self" (Naess, 1987, p. 35), which asserts that humans are interconnected with the entire web of life. This concept challenges the conventional view of the self as a separate entity from nature and encourages individuals to expand their sense of identity to encompass the entire biosphere (Naess, 1987, p. 37). "Self-realization," according to Naess, is the realization of entire biosphere, and the essence of deep ecology.

2.3.6 Ecofeminism

Ecofeminism, also called ecological feminism, is a socio-environmental movement that emerged in the late twentieth century as an intersectional philosophy that links the oppression of women and the exploitation of nature. This perspective places a strong emphasis on examining the treatment of both nature and women within a patriarchal, or male-centric, societal framework. It asserts that patriarchal (or male-centered) systems and environmental degradation are interconnected, and their roots lie in unjustified domination, objectification, and exploitation (Warren, 2000, p. 1).

One of the primary sources in the development of ecofeminism is the work of French feminist Françoise d'Eaubonne (1920-2005). In her 1974 book *Le Féminisme ou la Mort* (*Feminism or Death*), she coined the term "ecofeminism" and argued that the subjugation of women and the exploitation of the environment share common oppressive structures (d'Eaubonne, 2022, pp. 182–183).

Ecofeminism has since evolved, drawing from diverse feminist, environmental, and cultural perspectives. It continues to inspire activism and scholarship that challenge patriarchal and environmentally destructive practices, advocating for a more equitable and sustainable world.

2.3.7 Murray Bookchin's Social Ecology

Murray Bookchin (1920–2006), an American social theorist, historian, and political philosopher, is the founder of social ecology movement. His philosophy represents a transformative framework with considerable implications for sociopolitical and environmental discourse. Primarily expounded in his seminal work *The Ecology of Freedom: The Emergence and Dissolution of Hierarchy*, published in 1982, this perspective promotes the necessity of establishing a harmonious and sustainable relationship between "nature and humanity" (Bookchin, 1982, p. 11). It asserts that the fundamental origins of ecological and social crises are linked to hierarchical and exploitative social structures. For Bookchin, linked "with the social crisis is a crisis that has emerged directly from man's exploitation of the planet" (1982, pp. 18–19).

Central to Bookchin's framework is the advocacy for a paradigm shift, urging societies to transition away from hierarchical and oppressive systems toward decentralized and ecologically harmonious communities (Bookchin, 1982, p. 344). Furthermore, Bookchin's social ecology introduces the concept of liberation ecology, which underscores the intrinsic interdependence of social and environmental concerns. It contends that the emancipation of both humanity and the natural world is indispensable for forging a sustainable trajectory into the future (Bookchin, 1982, p. 176).

2.4 Critical Reflections on Environmentalism and the Need for a Theocentric Approach

The foregoing sections have illustrated disagreement and divergence in the positions among environmentalists about the human–nature relationship. The theories we have explored may appeal to some, but they are infested with several problems. There are, first, objections to "moral extensionism" on which the theories and approaches depend. Second, metaphysical and epistemological considerations have been overlooked, which are hard to suppress. Third, as many believe, the major contributing factor to the challenges faced in environmental ethics is taking for granted the foundational question of *who* is entitled to confer value on humans and other surrounding entities.

While recognizing the usefulness of different perspectives many scholars argue that secular-humanistic ethical frameworks, which dominate contemporary discourse, are inadequate to provide a comprehensive worldview grounded in metaphysical and epistemological traditions that prioritize accountability for and interdependence of nature. Consequently, there is a growing consensus that the fundamental questions raised in Section 2.2 need to be reassessed to effectively address pressing environmental concerns. As such, it is imperative to advocate for an alternative framework that may offer greater efficacy and practicality. The complex environmental crisis is thought by some to have resulted not only from political, economic, and social issues but also from religious, spiritual, moral, metaphysical, or philosophical crises (Özdemir, 2008).

To mitigate the environmental crisis, many believe that we need philosophical and religious understandings that recognize human beings as part of the natural world and dependent on ecological systems (Tucker & Grim, 2022). Thus, returning or reorienting humans to religious traditions is the key to solving the environmental crisis. This realization leads toward another system of beliefs and values – "theocentrism," a God-centered perspective.

3 Islam and Nature: Premodern Sources and Approaches

In the realm of Islamic thought and practice, a strong connection with nature has persisted over time. From Sufi perspective, emphasizing the divine reflections in the natural world, to practical environmental ethics in Islamic law, a holistic approach to ecological balance is evident. Early Muslim scholars addressed environmental issues, while pro-environmental practices, such as advanced water systems to aesthetic sensibilities, reflected a commitment to nature. The *Fiqh al-Bī'ah*, or Jurisprudence of the Environment, provides Islamic principles for conservation and ethical interaction with nature.

3.1 Sufi Writings on Nature

Sufism, a complex and diverse phenomenon, is a spiritual and mystical dimension within Islam, emphasizing inward search for a closeness to the divine. The word Sufism was coined during the Enlightenment; it stems from the root "ṣuf," with the European suffix "-ism" added in the eighteenth century. Though some see it as separate, mainstream Sufism is recognized as a diverse spiritual tradition within Islam, marked by varied ideas, literature, and rituals (Lings, 1975, pp. 11–16; Díaz, 2021, pp. 517–525). Sufi tradition provides a variety of expressions about nature since God and the natural world (the cosmos) have a strong relationship in Sufi thought. A prominent figure in this regard is the Andalusian Muḥyi al-Dīn ibn 'Arabī (1165–1240), who pioneered the concept of "unity of being" or "oneness of existence" (*waḥdat al-wujūd*), an idea which influenced many scholars throughout Islamic history (see Guessoum, 2011, p. 201). "God's self-manifestation" (*tajallī*) is central to Ibn 'Arabī's concept of *waḥdat al-wujūd*, which sees the relationship between Allah and the universe (cosmos) as one of unified existence. The underlying philosophy of this idea is that "the true existence is one and it is Allah's Existence" (Abrahamov, 2015, p. 6; Irawan, *et al.*, 2021). Ibn 'Arabī draws a parallel between humans, whom he refers to as a "microcosm" (*al-ʿālam al-ṣaghīr*), and nature, described as a "macrocosm" (*al-ʿālam al-kabīr*). According to Ibn 'Arabī's perspective, God manifests Himself in His creation, which encompasses the entire cosmos. As a result, he emphasizes the importance of showing deep respect and reverence for nature as an integral part of worshiping God. By recognizing the interconnectedness between humans and the natural world, individuals can strengthen their relationship with God and strive for inner purification, thus leading to positive transformations in both the spiritual and external realms (Irawan *et al.*, 2021).

In a similar vein, Jalāl al-Dīn Muḥammad Rūmī (1207–73), another illustrious Sufi and possibly the best-known Sufi master in the West, expressed deep love for nature in his poetry. For example, the best composition on nature, *Mathnavī* (a six-volume, epic-didactic poem) of Rūmī termed God's entire creation as alive. He writes, "Air, earth, water, and fire are God's servants. To us they seem lifeless, but to God living" (Clarke, 2003; Vaughan-Lee, 2013, p. 207). Rūmī expresses a deep connection between spirituality and nature in his poetry. He often refers to different natural entities, such as birds, rivers, oceans, trees, roses, horses, cows, the universe, and so on to represent spiritual symbols with the soul. His respect for and intimate relationship with nature signify his inner experiences (Whinfield, 2001; Irawan, *et al.*, 2021). Similarly, Farīd ad-Dīn 'Aṭṭār (d. 1220), in his *Manṭiq al-Ṭayr* (*The Conference of the Birds*), Persian "mystical poetry" in prose, exhibits a strong aesthetic taste for nature as expressed through his story of birds ('Aṭṭār, 1971).

Sufis had a strong connection to and love for nature because they could hear all of nature's prayers to God. This contemplative love for nature has, over the years, permeated Islamic society in its entirety. Traditional Islamic society has always been known for its harmonious relationship with nature and love for it, to the extent that many Christian critics of Islam have accused Muslims of being naturalists (Nasr, 1998, p. 123). The literature has long survived and continues to inspire Islamic ethicist commentators because it contains "elaborate classical allusions" (Setia, 2007, p. 141) to modern ecological concepts.

3.2 Premodern Muslim Intellectuals and Philosophers on Nature

While dealing with other sciences, several Muslim intellectuals also devoted many pages to various natural, environmental, and ecological issues. Environmental concerns such as environmental pollution and the protection and welfare of animals (Masri, 2007) have been explicitly articulated in Islamic history.

Environmental pollution, for example, as a cause of certain diseases, was discussed by Muslim scientists of the medieval period. Lutfallah Gari (2002), a Saudi scholar specializing in Islamic science and technology, explores twenty Arabic treatises (written up to the thirteenth century) investigating various dimensions of the environment, such as pollution and contagion, prevention of air and water pollution, the effects of weather, mishandling of solid waste, environmental assessment of specific cities, and so on. For example, al-Kindi's (d. 837) *Risālah fī 'īḍāḥ al-'llah fī al-Samā'im al-Qā'lah al-Samā'iyyah, wa Huwa 'Alā al-Qawl al-Mutlaq al-Wabā'* (*Causes of Heavenly Fatal Toxicants, Named Epidemics*) addresses issues related to environmental pollution and contagion. Qustā Ibn Lūqā's (d. 912) *Kitāb fī al-'I'dā'* (*On Contagion*) delves into the concept of contagion, describing it as the transmission from an unhealthy body to a healthier one. He proceeds to examine the methods of contagion and provides instances of communicable diseases. These discussions ultimately highlight two primary causes of widespread illness: the ambient air and infection. *Risālah fī al-Miyāh* (*Types of Waters*) of al- Rāzī (d. 925) describes different types of water from a physical point of view; al-Razi's *Risālah al-Wabā'iyyah* (*On Epidemics*) deals with environmental pollution and communicable diseases. Al-Tamīmī's (d. 1000) *Mādah al-Baqā' bi 'Iṣlāhi Fasād al-Hawā' wa al-Taḥarruz min Ḍarar al-Wabā'* (*Surviving Material about Treating Air Spoilage and Avoiding Epidemics*) discusses, among other topics, the categorization of polluted air types, the identification of diseases stemming from air pollution, hygienic measures aimed at disease prevention, incense varieties with air purification properties, and effective methods for handling stagnant water.

Ibn Sīnā (981–1037 CE) was a lesser-known environmental scientist better known in medicine and philosophy for his comprehensive and encyclopedic work *Kitāb al-Shifā'* (*The Book of Healing*). Also his *Qānūn* (*The Canon of Medicine*) holds great importance. It includes chapters covering diverse topics such as (i) the phenomenon of mouldiness; (ii) classification, characteristics, and purification methods of various types of water; (iii) diseases resulting from water impurity; (iv) the impact of air spoilage; (v) guidelines for designing houses and selecting their locations based on health considerations; (vi) the effects of food quality on health; and (vii) the role of animals in transmitting pollution or being observed during times of plague. Among other things, as noted by Gari, Ibn Sīnā remarked that, as a precursor to a looming plague, rats and subterranean creatures would emerge to the surface, exhibit signs of intoxication, and eventually die. Further exploration of these concepts can be found in Ibn Sīnā's work titled *Daf' al-Maḍār al-Kuliyyah 'An al-'Abdān al-Insāniyyah* (*Repelling General Harm from the Human Body*). The treatise extensively covers various forms of harmful air, including hot and cold air, coal smoke, perfumes, northerly and southerly winds, transitions between different air masses, epidemics resulting from air putrefaction, as well as stagnant and moving air. Additionally, the text delves into the identification and treatment of water-borne harms in reference to different types of water, such as forest water, saline water, bitter water, and sour water (Gari, 2002, pp. 480–481).

In Islamic culture, certain birds and animals would live harmoniously alongside humans. Muslim scholars were interested in featuring various animals simultaneously as metaphors and as real creatures in their literary and scientific writings (Gade, 2019, p. 170). For example, one of the best Arabic literary works, *Kalīlah wa Dimnah*, by a well-known eight-century scholar, Ibn Muqaffa', uses animals and birds as literary devices to convey moral lessons to adults and children (Atil, 1981) (its very title refers to the names of two jackals that feature as narrators and protagonists); the Andalusian Muslim scholar and polymath Ibn Ḥazm (994–1064) also uses birds as literary devices in his work *Ṭawq al-Ḥamāmah* (*The Ring of the Dove*) to convey his message about love and courtship, offering insights into the complexities of human relationships (Ḥazm, 1994). Similarly, a tenth-century Arabic fable, "The Case of the Animals versus Man Before the King of the Jinn," one of the epistles from *Rasā'il Ikhwān Al-Ṣafā'* (*Epistles of the Brothers of Purity*) of *Ikhwān Al-Ṣafā'* (*Brothers of Purity*), concerns a conflict between human beings and nature. It examines if humans are superior to animals and, if so, in what ways. Ibn Ṭufail (1105–85) a twelfth-century Arab Andalusian Muslim philosopher and polymath, best known for an Arabic philosophical novel, *Ḥayy Ibn Yaqẓān* (*Alive Son of Awake*), examines the animal–nature–human relationship in philosophical and spiritual perspectives.

In his influential work *Muqaddimah* (literally: *Introduction*), Ibn Khaldun (1332–1406 CE), a historian and philosopher, reflects on the impact of the physical environment on human history. He provides a comprehensive analysis of the intricate relationship between the natural environment, particularly the climate, and its profound influence on various aspects of human life. He expounds on how climatic conditions shape physical attributes, skin colouration, temperament, desires, societal customs, political dynamics, and economic activities of individuals and communities. For instance, due to the warm climate

> [t]he Egyptians are dominated by joyfulness, levity, and disregard for the future. They store no provisions of food, neither for a month nor a year ahead, but purchase most of it in the market. Fez in the Maghrib, on the other hand,

> lies inland and is surrounded by cold hills. Its inhabitants can be observed to look sad and gloomy and to be too much concerned for the future. Although a man in Fez might have provisions of wheat stored, sufficient to last him for years, he always goes to the market early to buy his food for the day, because he is afraid to consume any of his hoarded food. (Khaldun, 2005, p. 126)

Ibn Khaldun introduces a societal dichotomy, classifying people into two distinct types: nomadic and sedentary ones. He accords special significance to the nomadic populations who reside directly within the natural environment. In contrast, sedentary populations establish towns and cities that serve as epicenters of cultural refinement but are also susceptible to moral decadence. Additionally, he provides a comprehensive examination of the Earth's climatic zones. Interestingly, Ibn Khaldun espouses the view that overpopulation exerts a discernible impact on the quality of air (Khaldun, 2005, p. 390).

3.3 Premodern Pro-environmental Practices

Throughout Islamic history and culture, a range of pro-environmental practices have been identified, including the promotion of hygiene and health, the emphasis on cleanliness, the establishment of efficient water supply systems, the implementation of effective sanitation services, the management of waste, the prioritization of public safety, and the development of sustainable urban environments. These practices, deeply ingrained in Islamic traditions, demonstrate a long-standing commitment to the preservation and enhancement of the natural environment. Cleanliness and purity hold significant importance within Muslim society, as evidenced by the regular practice of purifying the body parts prior to the five daily prayers. This emphasis on cleanliness has driven the advancement of sophisticated bathhouses, hygienic toilets, and innovative engineering methods.

In medieval cities throughout the Islamic world, remarkable hydraulic-powered water supply systems were established, featuring an intricate network of dams, extensive irrigation systems, wells, aqueducts, and water canals known as *qanats*. These systems not only provided access to drinking water but also facilitated the abundance of water required for ritual ablutions in mosques and bathhouses. Muslims demonstrated ingenuity in water transportation, utilizing *qanats* to transport water over long distances, while large waterwheels known as *norias* (Figures 1 and 2) and donkey-driven water raising machines (Figure 3) facilitated the extraction of water from fast-flowing rivers and deep wells (UNESCO, 1977, p. 51; Al-Hassani, 2007, pp. 112–120).

Chant and Goodman, both scholars of the history of science and technology, observe that the urban water supply in Muslim cities was complemented by an efficient waste disposal system. Cities, including Baghdad, Damascus, Cordoba (Muslim Spain), Fez (Morocco), and Fustat (Egypt), featured well-developed waste disposal and sewage systems, characterized by interconnected networks of sewers. They elaborate on this point by noting that Cordoba had a network of sewers that extended from the upper city to the river, collecting waste waters from primary and secondary sources along the principal streets. These sewers,

Figure 1 *Norias* on the banks of Orontes River in the city of Hama, Syria.
Source: Al-Hassani (2007, p. 114).

Figure 2 *Norias* in Cordoba Spain.
Source: Nawaz (2019).

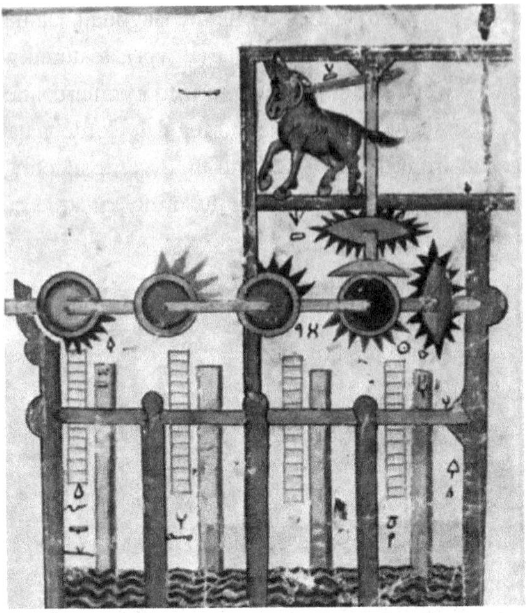

Figure 3 Donkey-driven irrigator.
Source: UNESCO (1977, p. 51).

constructed with limestone blocks and lined with concrete, were remarkably large, measuring up to two meters in width. The drainage system in medieval Fez was so effective that it was still utilized by French colonizers in the early twentieth century. Similarly, the city of Fustat, the capital of Muslim Egypt in the seventh century, exhibited an elaborate water supply and sewage disposal system that was thoughtfully designed to suit the local conditions (Chant & Goodmanm, 1999, p. 137; Haddad, 2021a).

Environmental concerns would also fully manifest through traditional Islamic architecture and city planning in sedentary environments for human and natural harmony, which was considered significant for its success. In the utilization of space, construction materials, water, sunlight and shade, heat and cold, wind, and gardens, special care was taken to maintain harmony and balance between humans and nature. Michell (2011, p. 201) observes that within the Islamic world, architecture serves as a strategic tool for regulating the environment in both hot and dry as well as hot and humid regions. A prevalent manifestation of this approach is observed in the design of courtyard houses, which effectively establish domestic microclimates. Islamic popular architecture, in particular, demonstrates an astute utilization of the insulation properties offered by various natural materials. A diverse array of ventilation systems was developed, showing an impressive level of sophistication in both conception and design. Moreover, the orientation of buildings in the Islamic world was carefully planned to facilitate optimal air circulation. This arrangement aimed to maximize the flow of air within the structure. Water was strategically channelled through the chambers, ultimately cascading down to the courtyards (Figure 4a–d). This design feature not only served to create

Figure 4(a) A private garden in Iran. Channels and pools constitute integral components of Islamic gardens. **(b)** Pool at Alhambra Granada. **(c)** Alhambra Granada. Water in directional sequence **(d)** Red Fort Delhi. Architecture design showing water enters building creating a soothing effect with sound, movement patterns, and cool breeze.

Source: Michell (2011, p. 156).

a prevailing cool breeze but also contributed to the overall thermal comfort of the building.

Islamic architecture not only displays a deep appreciation for aesthetic sensibilities but also reflects a sense of order inherent in nature and connects the worldly with the transcendent. For instance, the palace complex of Alhambra (Figure 5a–d), Spain, is renowned for its intricate geometric patterns, arabesques, and magnificent courtyards, demonstrating a sophisticated understanding of aesthetics and order. The Great Mosque of Cordoba (Figure 6), Spain, is another fabulous example of Islamic architecture in the Western world; the mosque features horseshoe arches, intricate mosaics, and a wonderful *mihrāb* (a niche), highlighting the beauty and order intrinsic to Islamic design. The Blue Mosque (Sultan Ahmed Mosque) (Figure 7), Istanbul, Turkey, known for its six minarets and blue tiles adorning the interior, is a masterpiece of Ottoman architecture, showcasing a harmonious blend of aesthetics and structural order. Similarly, the Registan Square (Figure 8) in Samarkand is surrounded by three grand madrasahs

Figure 5(a–c) Alhambra Palace, Spain.
(d) Tile decoration from the Alhambra Palace, Spain.

Source: Burckhardt (2009).

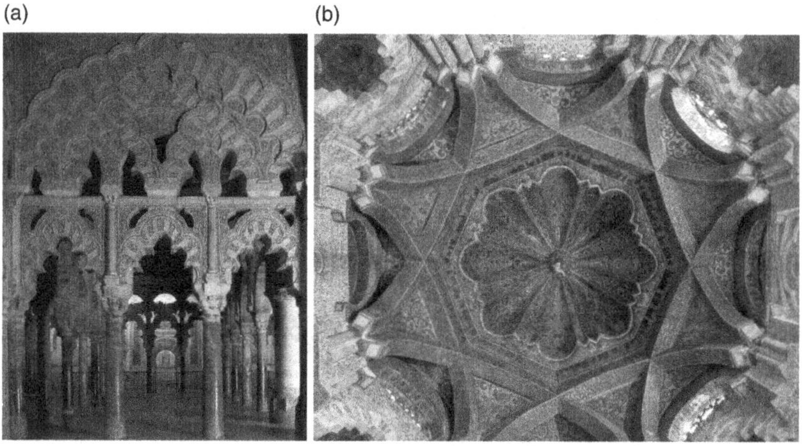

Figure 6a–b Interior of the Great Mosque of Córdoba. Area in front of the miḥrāb.

Source: Burckhardt (2009).

Figure 7 General view of the Sultan Ahmed Mosque, Istanbul, Turkey

Source: Burckhardt (2009).

adorned with ornate tiles and geometric patterns, illustrating the emphasis on symmetry and beauty in Islamic architectural design. The Taj Mahal (Figure 9), India, built in the Mughal architectural style, is a masterpiece of Islamic art. The symmetrical layout, intricate geometric patterns, and the use of calligraphy and

Figure 8 The Registan Square, Samarqand, Uzbekistan.

Source: Burckhardt (2009).

Figure 9a–b General view of the Taj Mahal, Agra, India. Main entrance to the shrine of the Taj Mahal.

Source: Burckhardt (2009).

floral motifs on the white marble reflect the Islamic principles of beauty, order, and the connection to the divine. Shāh Mosque (Figure 10a–b), Iṣfahān, Iran, is another prime example of Persian Islamic architecture. The intricate tilework, geometric patterns, and the vast courtyard showcase a meticulous attention to detail. The mosque's design is not only aesthetically pleasing but also

Figure 10a–b Dome of the Shāh Mosque at Iṣfahān
Source: Burckhardt (2009).

incorporates elements symbolizing the relationship between the earthly and the spiritual. For the intrinsic nature of architecture encompasses a symbolic conception that transcends mere aesthetic expression and spatial engagement, as observed by Elwazani (1995). Islamic architecture intricately weaves together the sacred traditions of the divine, harmonizing with the physical world to evoke a profound sense of order. Titus Burckhardt (1908–84), a German Swiss expert of Islamic art, architecture, and civilization, expresses that "[f]or a Muslim artist or ... a craftsman who has to decorate a surface, geometrical interlacement doubtless represents the most intellectually satisfying form, for it is an extremely direct expression of the idea of the Divine Unity underlying the inexhaustible variety of the world" (Burckhardt, 2009, p. 73). Thus, care for gardens and landscapes was a dominant feature of Muslim civilization (Nasr, 2020; Haddad, 2021b), the traces of which can still be found from Spain to India. Unfortunately, such practices are not visible in the contemporary Muslim societies.

3.4 *Fiqh al-Bī'ah* (Jurisprudence of the Environment)

The body of Prophetic traditions (sayings, doings, and tacit approval of the Prophet Muhammad) possesses numerous accounts that address issues such as the meaning and status of nature, livestock, agriculture, water resources, animals, birds, plants, land, and so on. Environmental concerns have also been profound and practical in Muslim legal thought.

The Qur'an and the Prophetic tradition form the basis of *Sharī'ah* and, thus, of Islamic environmental ethics that have been integrated within Islamic jurisprudence (*fiqh*) as Islamic environmental law. Many Muslim scholars, however, prefer using the term "Sharīʻah" to "law," for they maintain that "law" reflects "rigidity and dryness," which are alien to Islam (see Deen, 2004, p. 142). Therefore, before we deal with Islamic environmental law, it is relevant to understand what *Sharīʻah* is. *Sharīʻah* means at the same time "the way," "way to water," "the source of life," and "the law" (Llewellyn, 2003, p. 187; Deen, 2004, p. 142; Idllalène, 2021, pp. 8, 32), or the body or structure of those injunctions that Allah has ordained in their entirety or essence to lead individuals to Allah. *Sharīʻah* establishes standards for the orderly conduct of Muslims in all aspects of their lives, individually and collectively. Indeed, the science of ethics and that of Islamic law are the same. And it is more than just a religious doctrine, a law, or a legal system.

Islam does not recognize a rigid compartmentalization among law, morality, politics, and religion. As such, "the source of laws for water use and animal welfare are the same as for other aspects of human understanding and conduct. Thus, the literature on 'Islam and ecology', 'Islam and human rights', and 'Islam and animals' follows a general pattern. . . . In Islam this unified approach to thought and conduct is known as *Sharia'* or 'the way'" (Idllalène, 2021, p. 10). Consequently, it is challenging in Islamic and environmental law to separate the legal aspects from the ethical considerations. In Islam, legal changes do not occur in a vacuum but are accompanied by and embedded with moral force because "there is no division of ethics and law in Islam" (Sardar, 2006, p. 100; Gade, 2019, p. 118). Willis Jenkins (2005) argues that "a practical Islamic environmental ethics . . . may not first require a theology of nature, but an environmental jurisprudence" (p. 341).

Many scholars opine that there is a significant progressive environmental component in Islamic law as manifested in the sources of *Sharīʻah* – Qur'an, Ḥadīth, *Ijmā'* (consensus), *Qiyās* (analogical reasoning), and various environmental legal instruments – *ḥimā* (protected area or zone), *ḥarīm* (sanctuaries), *waqf* (endowment), *iqtā'* (land grant), *ijārah* (lease), *ihtikār* (hoarding), or *ḥisbah* (forbidding wrong/accountability) (Dien, 1996, p. 164; Haq, 2003, p. 128; Llewellyn, 2003; Idllalène, 2021, p. 33).

3.4.1 Ḥimā *(Reserves), and* Ḥarīm *(Inviolable Zones)*

The Prophetic traditions contain explicit norms of land allocation and conservation as reflected in the principles of *ḥimā* and *ḥarīm* (Hamed, 1993; Bagader, *et al.*, 1994; Dien, 2000). Both the related notions, literally meaning "protected" or "prohibited" and "reserved" areas, predate Islam (Al-ʻArabī, 1998, p. 72), but the Arab tribal chieftains would not allow others to enter the protected area while grazing their animals. The Prophet Muhammad (Al-Bukhārī, *Ṣaḥīḥ al-Bukhārī*, Book 42, Ḥadīth 2370, 1997, p. 320) prohibited this practice. While the *ḥadīths* affirm the right to private property, it also recognizes public ownership of essential resources like water, pasture, and fire (Dāwūd, *Sunan Abū Dāwūd*, Book 22, Ḥadīth 3477, 2008, pp. 129–130). The Prophet Muhammad established these resources, including forests, as communal assets, abolishing private reserves that were used by the Arab aristocracy to claim exclusive rights to best grazing lands for their personal use (Qudāmah, 1997, p. 165).

Islam promoted the institution of *ḥimā*, which was the establishment of public reserves dedicated to the conservation and production of resources, such as woody vegetation, wildlife, and horses for the Muslim army. This practice aimed to protect these natural assets and ensure their sustainable use for the benefit of the community. It abolished pre-Islamic practices and incorporated the "religious values and norms . . . into the *Hima* system. The function of the *Hima* changed and became property dedicated to the wellbeing of the community around it" (Gari, 2006, p. 213). According to Peter Vincent, "The *Hima*, as a system, is possibly the oldest known organized form of conservation [in] the world" (Setia, 2007, p. 133). Owing to its ecological, social, and economic implications, The Prophet Muhammad is reported to have transformed the *ḥimā* from a private property into a public asset (Idllalène, 2021, p. 51) and "[laid] down the rules by which it came to be one of the essential instruments of conservation in Islamic law" (Llewellyn, 2003, p. 212).

Moreover, the Prophet declared and preserved the surroundings of Makkah and Madīnah, a sanctuary representing the two primordial inviolable sanctuaries (*al-ḥaramain*) where hunting was forbidden within a radius of four miles (Llewellyn, 2003, p. 212). Similarly, the destruction of trees and shrubs was also made illegal within twelve miles. In a *ḥadīth*, the Prophet Muhammad emphasized: "If I were to find deer in the territory between the two mountains, I would not molest them, and he (the Prophet Muhammad) declared twelve miles of suburb around Medina as a prohibited pasture" (Muslim, *Ṣaḥīḥ Muslim*, Book 15, Ḥadīth 1372, 2007, p. 520). He also established Al-Naqī' (Al-Bukhārī, *Ṣaḥīḥ al-Bukhārī*, Book 42, Ḥadīth 2370, 1997, p. 320), one of the first *ḥimās* in Islamic law, near Madīnah for the protection of wildlife and vegetation. He prohibited private reserves for exclusive use by an individual (Sardar, 2006, p. 103). In this way, the Prophet instituted a kind of what would be today called a "national park" (Nasr, 2020, pp. 158–159) or "zonation of land," which were considered "safe zones" (Idllalène, 2021), where flora and fauna received special protection.

The caliphs (successors of the Prophet) continued the practice and designated more areas under the *ḥimā* system. Caliph 'Umar is reported to have "established additional *himās* for the cavalry, the camels allocated to charity and the livestock of the poor" (Llewellyn, 2003, p. 212). Consequently, *ḥimā* and *ḥarīm* emerged as a "flexible conservation management system that enables the establishment of land and marine conservation zones in designated areas" (Khalid, 2017, p. 141).

In modern times, a specialized field of Islamic jurisprudence, known as *Fiqh of Bī'ah* (Jurisprudence of Environment), emerged. It encompasses a set of principles derived from Islamic sources that guide our actions toward a conservationist approach. The extensive collection of *ḥadīth* and Islamic legal texts (see Taymiyyah, 1965; Yūsuf, 1979; Qudāmah, 1997) includes substantial content pertaining to land, water, pasture, and other environmental issues, categorized under the branch of "*mu'āmalāt*" (transactions). For example, in his book *Kitāb al-Kharāj* (*The Book of Taxation*), Abū Yūsuf (731–798) writes in detail about the revival of the dead Earth (*Ihya' al-mawāt*). Similarly, Ibn Taymiyyah (1263–1328), in his magnum opus, *Majmū' al-Fatāwā*, writes that "hunting solely for the purpose of amusement and play is disliked (*makrūh*). If such hunting involves harming people by trespassing on their farms or damaging their property, then it is considered prohibited (*ḥarām*)" (1965, p. 619).

Haq (2001a, pp. 119–129; 2001b, pp. 149–150; 2003, pp. 141–150) provides an in-depth examination of the material on *Fiqh of Bī'ah* mentioned in the corpus of *ḥadīth* and *fiqh*. It addresses issues such as land management and ownership, pastures, fuel wood, and water. In addition, a system of land grants, charitable endowments (*awqāf*), and an office of public inspection (*iḥtisāb/muḥtasib*) was established during the era of the second caliph, 'Umar (634–644) (Al-Bar, 1992, p. 549), for the proper functioning of *mu'āmalāt*-a prototype of environmental jurisprudence. *Ḥisbah*, the Islamic concept of market supervision, has remained a constant feature of Muslim society, especially during the medieval times with the purpose of promoting goodness and eradicating evil within society (Al-Maqrīzī, 1971, p. 395; Al-Maydānī, 1998, p. 632). Moreover, a classical Muslim scholar, 'Izz al-Dīn 'Abd al-Salām (1181-1262) offers essential and exhaustive jurisprudential insights about animal rights in his book *Qawā'id al-Aḥkām fī Maṣāliḥ al-An'ām* (*Rules for Judgment in the Cases of Living Beings*) (2015). Given its flexibility and relevance to evolving contemporary circumstances, the *Fiqh of Bī'ah* is regarded by Muslim environmentalists and legal experts as a promising legal framework for environmental conservation.

4 Islam and Nature: The Modern Discourse

Before delving systematically into the Islamic theocentric approach, it is crucial to provide a concise overview of the emergence of Islamic environmental discourse, commonly labeled as "eco-theology." It is, however, important to add that eco-theology is not necessarily limited to any specific religious tradition, including Islam. Eco-theology explores the relationship between religion, spirituality, and the environment, addressing questions about how religious beliefs and teachings relate to ecological concerns, environmental ethics, and the stewardship of the natural world. It can take different forms within different religious contexts and may vary in its theological interpretations and practices. That having been said, eco-theology serves as the theoretical foundation for the Islamic principles of environmental ethics in modern era.

4.1 The Three Approaches

Over the last fifty years, the literature on ecological conservation and environmental protection produced by Muslim environmentalists, especially those living in the West, has been commendable. However, Muslim environmentalism only became a prominent academic trend post-2000 (DeLong-Bas, 2018), influenced by a broader environmental movement that emerged in the West. The scholarship heavily draws from rereading the Qur'an and Sunnah (traditions) of the Prophet Muhammad, with some attention to Islamic *Sharī'ah* law. The body of literature gives an understanding of Islamic norms of the environment that could be broadly referred to as "the discourse of eco-theology," for it is based on Islamic transcendental principles.

The Islamic environmentalist discourse is not uniform. Some ideas are common, but their focus, approach, methodology, and emphasis differ. Generally, a scriptural-religious approach is predominant, followed by an ethical one. Philosophical and legal methodologies are also part of Islamic environmentalism. It is also worth mentioning that in the discourse of Islam and ecology, there exists a debate over what constitutes "Islamic" in the Islam and ecology discourse. Richard Foltz, a Canadian scholar known for his work in the fields of history, religion, and environment, distinguishes between Islamic texts and Muslim practices; he views that we should be cautious in differentiating between "Islamic" and "Muslim," while prefixing with "environmentalism," for every action of a Muslim does not necessarily represent or substantiate Islam. Islamic environmentalism, Foltz emphasizes, draws from the textual sources of Islam (Foltz, 2003, p. 252). He adds that contemporary environmental activism, both in theory and practice, functions in various frameworks and operates among diverse people and establishments across the globe. For example, the environmental programs of the UK-based organization IEEFS (discussed in Section 6.1) draw from the textual sources of Islam. On the other hand, Muslim international environmental organizations like the IUCN and WWF tend to follow Western ideas of "what constitutes environmental education and protection," even if they are run by Muslim staff in Muslim countries like Egypt, Pakistan, and Indonesia (Foltz, 2005b, p. 859).

Bagir and Martiam (2017, p. 80) contend that Foltz's distinction between Islam and Muslim environmentalism is problematic, for they assert that it is challenging to come up with ideas or interpretations that are universally acceptable to Muslims as "Islamic," except for some fundamental issues, because Muslims are not culturally immune. Thus, their practices would be culturally influenced, yet "they do not have to be rejected as 'un-Islamic'" (p. 85). Based on this rationale, the Muslim approach represents a spectrum of ideas about the environmental crisis, which is divided into the following approaches: scriptural-theological, ethical- philosophical or mystical, and legal.

A popular trend in Islamic discourse on environmental concerns is a scriptural-religious approach. The principal characteristic of this position is based on the exposition of how Islamic tradition, especially the two primary sources, the Qur'an and *ḥadīth*, "has actually been or has the potential to be a 'green religion'" (Bagir & Martiam, 2017, p. 80). The scholars of this trend generally do not go deep to interpret the textual references, for they believe the occurrences of references speak for themselves about environmental concerns. This approach reflects some broad common themes which cut across the writings of Muslim environmentalists. *Tawḥīd* (the oneness of God), the concept of "unity in creation"; *khilāfah*, or human' stewardship on the Earth; and *ākhirah*, which entails human responsibility and accountability to God in the hereafter, are three major themes that are illustrative of this exposition (see, Zaidi, 1981; Manzoor, 1984; Zaman, 1986; Bagader *et al.*, 1994; Wersal, 1995). We shall take a closer look at such concepts in Section 5. Although textual (normative) sources are integral to any Islamic environmental understanding, some view that mere citations of these sources or precepts would not be enough unless, at the very least, they reshape perceptions regarding the status of nature (Bagir & Martiam, 2017, p. 80). Major Muslim environmental commentators provide an outline of foundational source materials to extend their scope to environmental conservation.

An ethical concern of Islam and ecology is the most recurrent theme in Islamic environmentalism. Many Muslim commentators and thinkers attempt to derive environmental ethical principles based on the Qur'an and Sunnah. For Adi Setia (2007), an environmental problem is an "attitude problem, not a resource problem"; therefore, changing one's moral and behavioral attitude toward the environment is essential. Muslim environmentalists maintain that the environmental crisis is a spiritual and religious crisis brought about by the modern scientific worldview of nature. Thinkers such as Seyyed Hossein Nasr, Fazlun Khalid, and Tariq Ramadan have identified the root cause of the current ecological crisis, attributing it to the materialistic and modern scientific worldview of nature prevalent in the West. We shall examine their respective views in more detail in Sections 4.1.1–4.1.5.

Other eminent contemporary scholars, including Mawil Izzi Dien and Uthman Llewellyn (discussed in Section 4.1.3), offer environmental law or jurisprudence as a practical tool for ecological conservation. They maintain that nonbinding legal opinions to the environment are more explicit in *fiqh* literature than in the Qur'an and *ḥadīth* (the two fundamental texts of *fiqh*). *Fatāwā*, nonbinding legal rulings, demonstrate how the environment is seen as a moral issue with a religious solution based on social justice (Gade, 2019, p. 145).

4.1.1 Seyyed Hossein Nasr

Let's take a closer look at the influential contributions of Seyyed Hossein Nasr (b. 1933), which include his lecture series titled "The Encounter of Man and Nature," delivered at the University of Chicago in 1966. Such lectures served as a catalyst for raising awareness and stimulating a deeper understanding of the ecological challenges from an Islamic standpoint among the Muslim community. They were later published in the form of a book, *Man and Nature: The Spiritual Crisis in Modern Man* (1968). Nasr has been a part of the discourse about Islam and the environment in the years since, being a very productive author in the field.

In the book *Religion and the Order of Nature* (1996), Nasr argues that the spiritual crisis underlies the modern environmental problems. The book explores environmental concerns within the context of religious perspectives and serves as a rallying call for "traditional believers" to unite in the defense of nature. Nasr links the present environmental problems to the moral and spiritual crisis of the modern world brought about by the obsession with scientism that confronts traditional norms and values (Nasr, 1975). Moreover, he attributes Muslims' obliviousness to the environment to Western influence and interference in Muslim countries (Nasr, 1997, 2003). Interestingly, Nasr's engagement with environmental concerns predates the aforementioned 1967 controversial article by Lynn White, "The Historical Roots of Our Ecological Crisis," which blamed Christianity, particularly, for the present environmental crisis.

According to Nasr (1968, pp. 18–19), "the sense of domination over nature and a materialistic conception of nature on the part of modern humans are combined, moreover, with a lust and sense of greed which makes an even greater demand upon the environment." Nasr further asserts that "the sciences of nature lost their symbolic intelligibility, a fact that is most directly responsible for the crisis which the modern scientific world view and its applications have brought about" (1968, p. 21). Therefore, he promotes for a significant transformation in how we perceive the natural world, advocating a paradigm shift away from the prevailing scientific outlook and toward a more traditional, religious, and spiritual understanding of nature (Nasr, 1968, pp. 118–119). According to Nasr, the ecological crisis can only be effectively addressed through a radical transformation of the prevailing mechanistic-materialistic view of the natural world (Nasr, 1968, pp. 7, 21–22). He argues that this shift is essential for achieving long-term ecological sustainability, emphasizing the need to embrace a spiritual and participatory understanding of nature.

Additionally, since the late 1960s, Nasr has been calling for a renewed philosophical interpretation of nature as "sacred," drawing from the perennial philosophy (Foltz, 2006a; Mary, 2006; Johnston, 2012). Nasr emphasizes it in his book, *Religion and the Order of Nature*: "a nexus must be created in this realm among the traditions, as has been carried out by the traditional proponents of the perennial philosophy for the understanding of the Divine Principle and its numerous manifestations in various religious universes" (Nasr, 1996, p. 7). However, a vast majority of Muslims have not accepted his philosophical interpretation, especially of "nature." Nasr's eco-theological suggestions have been criticized for lacking practical solutions and clear alternatives to the modern lifestyle. Some find his esoteric narratives and mystic descriptions difficult to comprehend (Sayem, 2019, pp. 294–295).

In Islam, ethical concerns have religious underpinnings and thus have a tremendous role to play in changing the behavior of humans toward the environment and other nonhuman animals. Enjoining what is good (*ma'rūf*) and forbidding what is wrong (*munkar*) have been the hallmarks of this approach. It reiterates adhering to such ideals as moderation, compassion, and justice. Some have argued against this thesis, saying that ethics alone are not enough to reshape people's perception and attitude toward nature because not everyone follows ethics, no matter how strong and appealing the ethics are (Ouis, 1998, p. 177; Jenkins, 2005, p. 342). That being the case, again, Nasr's shortcoming has been ignoring *Sharī'ah* or legal dimensions in projecting his perspective on environmental ethics. Therefore, it is often argued that ethical considerations without Islamic legal rulings will not substantially change people's behavior toward the environment.

That having been said, Nasr's philosophical and spiritual insights do contribute to a deeper understanding of the ecological crisis within the context of faith and spiritual traditions. While there may be limitations and a need for more practical proposals, Nasr successfully connects the ecological crisis to broader philosophical and spiritual considerations.

4.1.2 Fazlun Khalid

Fazlun Khalid (b. 1932), Sri Lankan-born and founder of a prominent Birmingham-based environmental organization, is one of the most vocal authors on the ecological problems stemming from modern science, and has been called "the foremost expert on ecology from the Islamic perspective" (Sharp, 2015, p. 471).

Khalid views that the "seeds of the ecological crisis that breached these limits were sown during the period that followed the Renaissance ... [resulting from T]he shift in humankind's perception of itself in relation to the natural order. This is encoded in what has now come to be known as the secular scientific worldview" (Khalid, 2003, p. 301), which occurred from the sixteenth century onward when what we now know as "modernity" began to "evolve" (Khalid, 2003, p. 307). What was more disappointing, according to Khalid, was the enticement of consumerism and the creation of an artificial sense of prosperity that this prevailing paradigm has led to the brink of an imminent ecological disaster. Khalid says: "[w]e now exist in soulless secularized spaces, concealing the reality that we are all trapped in an irresistible undertow of debt and hedonism aimlessly driving us through oceans of consumerism" (Khalid, 2019, p. 39). He connects "secularized spaces" and consumerism with the wider crises that humanity is going through.

The first organized presentation of the Islamic position on environmental protection was a short treatise titled "Islamic Principles for the Conservation of the Natural Environment," published in 1983 by the Saudi Meteorology and Environmental Protection Administration (MEPA) and the International Union for the Conservation of Nature (IUCN). The paper produced, however, was poorly publicized. Similarly, other Muslim organizations also played a pivotal role in Islamic environmentalism. For example, the Islamic Foundation for Ecology and Environmental Sciences (IFEES), established in 1993 in Birmingham, England, by Khalid, is one of the most active organizations spreading environmental awareness by organizing workshops, community engagements, and educational programmes in many Muslim countries. The organization launched the world's first Islamic conservation guide in 2008 in Zanzibar. We will take a closer look at this in Section 6.

4.1.3 Mawil Y. Izzi Dien and Uthman Llewellyn

The Iraqi Mawil Y. Izzi Dien (b. 1948: also known as Izzi Deen) is the first contemporary Muslim scholar to write about how Islamic law can be used to solve today's environmental problems. He has been vocal in projecting the management and distribution of natural resources according to Islamic jurisprudence. A significant portion of his book, *The Environmental Dimensions of Islam* (2000), focuses on the use of Islamic law along with a moral ethic in ecology. He is more concerned about the legal tool of *maṣlaḥah*, an important concept in Islamic legal theory, which encompasses the principles of utility (*maṣlaḥah*) and the broader objectives of Islamic law (*maqāṣid al-sharīʻah*). Commonly used by contemporary Muslim reformers, *maṣlaḥah* serves as a guiding principle for proposing legal reforms and addressing contemporary challenges. Broadly understood as "welfare," jurists utilize *maṣlaḥah* to denote the "general good" or "public interest," emphasizing its role in averting harm and promoting human well-being (Khadduri, 2012). In the Islamic legal and ethical framework, according to *maṣlaḥah*, when the interests of individuals and specific groups cannot be reconciled with the broader interests of society as a whole, the latter takes precedence. The collective welfare and well-being of society are given priority over the individual and particular group interests. This recognition acknowledges the need for harmonization and balance, ensuring that decisions and actions prioritize the greater common good rather than catering solely to individual or limited group interests. Similarly, a sub-maxim of Islamic legal rule is when a situation of a conflict between harm and benefit arises in executing an action, the avoidance of harm takes precedence over the pursuit of benefits (*dar' al-mafāsid awlā min jalb al-maṣāliḥ*) (Al-Zuḥaylī, 2006, p. 238). This principle arises from the strong emphasis in Islamic law on abstaining from forbidden actions rather than focusing solely on permissible ones. Moreover, the allowance for pursuing benefits is primarily justified as a means of preventing harm, as refraining from beneficial actions can often lead to inflicted harm. Thus, the guiding principle emphasizes prioritizing the prevention of harm in decision-making and prioritizing actions. By upholding this principle, ethical considerations can guide decision-making processes that contribute to the overall welfare and harmony of society. Elaborating on the legal principle of public benefit, Dien (2000, p. 136) writes:

> This principle can be extended to many contemporary environmental threats since they are potentially greater killers than any homicidal individual, and the interest achieved, in both avoiding and removing them, is often unquestionable, even if there is the loss of benefits expected from them. Islamic legislation is expected to have provisions to protect the environment and guarantee its sustainability.

While Dien offers a detailed exploration of the Islamic perspective on environmentalism, Islamic ethics, and the use of Islam legal tools in ecology, he falls short in providing practical examples that illustrate the application of Islamic legal principles to address contemporary environmental crises. Nonetheless, Izzi Dien's environmental approach involves employing the Islamic legal principle of *maṣlaḥah*, where he emphasizes that environmental threats jeopardize human life, aligning with the objectives of *Sharīʻah*. Additionally, Dien advocates for the application of *maṣlaḥah* to avoid harm, asserting that Islamic legislation should include provisions to protect the environment and ensure sustainability. This underscores his view of integrating Islamic legal tools to address environmental challenges, safeguarding both human well-being and the broader objectives of *Sharīʻah*. He accepts that traditional *fiqh* experiences "remain historically distant from contemporary application without careful analysis of the concepts which they provide" (2000, p. 49). So, he views that "[t]he conservation of the natural environment in Islam is both an ethical and a religious imperative which should be backed with legislation and effective enforcement of an environmental law" (Dien, 2000, p. 282). He asserts that the jurisprudence of *fiqh* needs reshaping to make it viable in line with modern ecological problems, for it offers "pragmatic resources" to initiate changes within the social structure (Jenkins, 2005).

Similarly, Uthman Abd al-Rahman Llewellyn's "Basis for a Discipline of Islamic Environmental Law" (2003) explores the potential of Islamic *fiqh* rulings in resolving environmental problems. He is optimistic that traditional *fiqh* corpus contains many injunctions and institutions, particularly for regulating and protecting natural resources. Like Dien, Llewellyn displays particular interest in exploring the environmental functions of past institutions such as *ḥimā* (inviolable zone), *ḥarīm* (reserve land), and *waqf* (endowment), which offer valuable opportunities for the contemporary advocates of animal rights, theorists, and policymakers (Llewellyn, 2003; Jenkins, 2005; Johnston, 2012).

Llewellyn relies on Islamic legal traditions and elaborates on their application to the environmental crisis in modern times; however, he acknowledges the challenges that many of them face on the ground. He presents an interdisciplinary collaborative approach between environmental experts and Muslim jurists, which is indispensable in the modern context, especially in Muslim-majority countries:

> The problem is that environmental law requires not only legal rulings and precedents from centuries gone by or ideal statements of general principle but creative, practical, detailed application of these precedents and principles to specific environmental, socioeconomic, and technological problems. In other words, it requires *ijtihad*. (Llewellyn, 2003, p. 237)

Izzi Dien and Uthman Abd al-Rahman Llewellyn advocate for utilizing Islamic jurisprudence to address environmental challenges. Dien emphasizes reshaping traditional fiqh, employing *maṣlaḥah* (utility), and treating environmental conservation as an ethical and religious imperative. In contrast, Llewellyn proposes adapting fiqh to contemporary needs through flexible interpretations and interdisciplinary collaboration, offering a solution within Islamic legal principles. Together, their approaches promote the integration of Islamic legal tools for effective and adaptable environmental solutions grounded in ethical *Sharīʿah* principles. The growing interest in the Islamic legal aspects of environmental conservation reflects an evolving discourse that emphasizes the legal frameworks and interdisciplinary approaches. Scholars are increasingly recognizing the protection of the natural environment as one of the objectives (*maqāṣid*) of *Sharīʿah*, as highlighted by a prominent Islamic scholar, Yūsuf al-Qaraḍāwī (1926–2022). Integrating environmental concerns into the *Maqāṣid al-Sharīʿah* discourse is seen as a natural extension of the Islamic legal approach (Kamali, 2016). The utilization of land, water, plants, and animals is examined in light of the ultimate objectives of Islamic law (Llewellyn, 1985), displaying the flexibility of Islamic legal discourse and its practical application to environmental issues. The case of Indonesia serves as an interesting example, where ecological preservation has been given legal priority, reflecting the recognition of the importance of environmental conservation within the Muslim context (Bagir & Martiam, 2017).

4.1.4 Other Notable Contributions

Tariq Ramadan (b. 1962) advocates for a reformation of our modern unbridled economic outlook to preserve the environment. He emphasizes that "[n]ature suffers because of some forms of human behavior. This is mainly due to the way of life of some societies, the richest and most industrialized, which squander natural resources, pollute the planet, deplete the ozone layer, and produce astounding amounts of greenhouse gases" (Ramadan, 2009, p. 253). What is needed according to Ramadan is "to reform our general approach of problems, our ways of life, our modes of consumption, and our relationship to human solidarity; in other words, our fundamental education" (Ramadan, 2009, p. 253). Furthermore, according to Ramadan, "[t]he profoundly moral content of the Qur'an and the eminently ethical nature of the Prophet's exemplary life provide the central elements for understanding the Islamic message" (Ramadan, 2018, p. 5). He emphasizes that "the Universe is in fact a Revelation that must be respected, read, understood, and protected, [we] should reform our minds and our attitudes toward nature, animals, and therefore also to an economy focused on economic production and the mad logic of economic growth at all costs to society" (Ramadan, 2009, p. 234).

A significant advancement in the Islam and ecology discourse matured in 1998, when forty Muslim scholars, activists, and politicians from around the world participated in a conference titled "World Religions and Ecology" organized at Harvard University. In 2003, the papers were put together in a book called *Islam and Ecology: A Bestowed Trust*. As of 2024, it is the most extensive collection of Muslim writings on Islam and the environment.

One of the most influential contemporary Islamic thinkers on animal rights is an Indian-born Bashir Ahmad Masri (1914–93). His book *Animal Welfare in Islam*, originally published as *Animals in Islam* in 1988 and later republished under its current title in 2007, represents a significant and valuable contribution.

M. Gade's *Muslim Environmentalism: Religious and Social Foundations* (2009) explores historical and modern theoretical developments in Muslim environmentalism and pushes for environmental humanities. Gade is innovative in that, unlike other environmental scholars, she focuses on projecting Muslim environmentalism as a broad humanities discipline.

5 Principles of Islamic Environmental Ethics: A Systematic-Prescriptive Exploration

5.1 Islamic Theocentrism

The Islamic perspective on nature is neither ecocentric nor anthropocentric but is fundamentally "theocentric" (God-centered) (Ahmad, 1997; Foltz, 2006a; Watling, 2009; Bratton, 2021). According to a theocentric view, everything, including human beings, has value in *relation* to and with the One and Only God. Humans, though, enjoy a special status in this scheme of life, and they are enjoined to use the natural world to fulfill their welfare.

Critics argue that theocentrism entails anthropocentrism, for it encourages human exceptionalism and makes humans the overlords of the entire Earth and all other myriad forms of biological life (Bratton, 2021, p. 21). To this, the advocates of theocentrism respond that their position in no way gives humankind unlimited and unbridled rights and access to natural resources: "this dominion facilitates stewardship and need not involve domination, recklessness and ruthlessness" (Attfield, 2001, p. 96). It comes with moral and ethical responsibilities coupled with human answerability to God for his actions (Attfield, 1999, p. 45; 2017, p. 149; Bratton, 2021, p. 21).

In general, all the world's religious traditions possess ethical concerns, though there may be differences, for the natural world and fairness to fellow human beings. Islam has unique considerations and directions about what sort of human–nature relationship there should be. Although Islam does not have a specific doctrine concerning the environment, it does have a doctrine concerning "man's duty to

Allah, to his fellows, and to the world that encompasses everything relevant to the question" (Hobson, 1998, p. 36). Within Islam, an inclusive worldview is projected wherein human beings, the environment, and the universe are perceived as interconnected entities characterized by a synchronized, balanced, and harmonious relationship, guided by "celestial" or "supernatural" principles (Nasr, 1996, pp. 223, 272).

Furthermore, character development holds significant importance in Islam. This can be observed through the ultimate objective of the mission of the Prophet Muhammad, as stated in a *ḥadīth*, which is "to perfect good character" (Mālik, *Muwaṭṭa'*, Book 47, Ḥadīth 8, 2014, p. 679). This outlook brings us to an important understanding of the reality and meaning of life. Muslims believe that the purpose and meaning of life lie in one's devotion and submission to Allah (God). Subsequent to this belief is the adherence to Islamic principles, the pursuit of spiritual growth, and the cultivation of righteousness. Muslims view life as a test, wherein individuals are tasked with upholding moral virtues and seeking proximity to Allah.

The belief in the One Creator and life in the hereafter serve as the central axis around which the ethical norms of the Qur'an revolve. Disregarding these two axioms, whether consciously or unconsciously, affects spiritual growth and development and destroys individual motivation to do good. John Kaltner (2011, p. 47) summarizes the position of the Islamic worldview on the human–nature relationship. For Muslims, he writes:

> Everything is dependent upon God for its existence and . . . [t]hat may explain why some scholars have that *tawḥīd*, or unity, is the starting point for Islamic understanding of the environment. If all is created by God, and God is one, it follows that there is a unity and connectedness within creation.

Islamic ethics and morality have profound environmental implications, advocating integrity, fairness, and uprightness not only in personal matters but also in socioeconomic concerns, regardless of time and space constraints. The Qur'an and the Prophetic traditions offer a wide range of ethical principles, directives, and values for individual problems, societal and state policy, and global ecological problems (Mortada, 2003; Ahmad, 2009, p. 93). A close look into the contents and themes of the Qur'an and the Prophetic traditions reveals frequent references to nature and pro-environmental concepts. This might have been the main motivation for many premodern Muslim thinkers (see Section 3) to give particular focus to nature and pro-environmental practices.

5.2 Islamic Scriptures and Nature

The Islamic description of nature is primarily reflected in the Qur'an and takes many forms; it is further approached and explained in the Prophetic traditions and still delved into deeply in later Islamic environmental literature. However, neither the word "nature" nor any reference to "environment" or its "isms" is found in the Qur'an. The closest term in modern Arabic usage, which gives the meaning of "habitat" or "surroundings," is *bī'ah* (see Khalid, 2019, p. 169). Nonetheless, the essential teachings of the Qur'an implicitly direct attention to environmental concepts, given the frequent references to nature. More than 750 verses in the Qur'an mention various aspects of the natural world (Shomali, 2008). In addition, the Arabic word for creation, that is, *khalq*, is mentioned in 250 verses of the Qur'an. That is why Bassett *et al.* (2000, p. 56) held that "[k]nowledge of creation is the basis for environmental teachings in the Qur'an."

Interestingly, fourteen chapters in the Qur'an are named after various creatures and phenomena in nature. Some of these chapters include the cow, the cattle, the thunder, the bee, the ant, the daybreak, the sun, the night, the fig, the elephant, the spider, and the star. These references within Islamic texts serve to underscore the profound significance of nature, necessitating meticulous contemplation. They signal that nature has a role that extends beyond mere existence: It is something to be respected, nurtured, and cared for, and it has a purpose in the broader ethical and spiritual context of Islamic teachings. These references prompt readers and adherents to recognize the intrinsic value of the natural world and to understand that their actions should reflect a sense of stewardship and responsibility toward it.

In sum, nature holds paramount significance in Islam. It is important to emphasize, however, that Islam does not ascribe divinity or sacredness to nature; rather, nature is regarded as part of the intricate web of creation, alongside all other living beings within the universe. The Qur'an declares: "There is no God but He, the Creator of all things" (Quran An'ām/6:102).[1] This belief in the Oneness of God is the fundamental principle (we will come back to this later) that frames Islamic understanding of nature and connects it to the divine but does not make it divine.

The term *āyāt* (signs) in the Qur'an is used to denote various elements in the natural world. On several occasions, the Qur'an describes many natural events as divine signs (*āyāt Allah*) reflecting Allah's knowledge, wisdom, and might, or proof of the divine, such as:

> (To guide) those who use their reason (to this Truth) there are many Signs in the structure of the heavens and the earth, in the constant alternation of night

[1] In this Element, unless otherwise stated, all translations of the Qur'anic verses will be from Abul A'lā Mawdūdī, *Towards Understanding the Qur'an* [English version of *Tafhīm al-Qur'ān*], tr. and ed., Zafar Isḥāq Anṣārī, (New Delhi: MMI, 2013).

> and day, in the vessels which speed across the sea carrying goods that are of profit to people, in the water which Allah sends down from the sky and thereby quickens the earth after it was dead, and disperse over it all manner of animals, and in the changing courses of the winds and the clouds pressed into service between heaven and earth. (Qur'an Baqarah/2: 164)

> There are many Signs on earth for those of sure faith. And also in your own selves. Do you not see? (Qur'an Dhāriyāt/51: 20-21)

These understandings – that the entire universe or cosmos is, in fact, a "revelation" – must be followed by respect – comprehend, ponder, and protect. Moreover, as the cosmic revelation, the natural world represents the power and majesty of the Creator. Thus, for many Muslim environmental ethicists, the view of creation as signs of Allah (*āyāt Allah*) is the most solid legal basis for environmental conservation and protection (Nasr, 1992; Bagader *et al.*, 1994; Dien, 2000; Llewellyn, 2003; Ramadan, 2009). William A. Graham (2016, p. 116) elaborates on this concept:

> The use of the same word, *āyah*, both for a single unit of revelation, or "verse," of the Qur'ān and for any one of the natural "tokens," "portents," or "signs" of the divine found so abundantly in nature, is not merely a coincidence of language; nor is it accidental that *āyah* can also mean "wonder" or "miracle." Rather, this usage signals that just as God's revealed scripture is a book of God's "signs" (or "miracles") to be recited/read as a "reminder" (*dhikr*), so God's created world is itself a kind of "book" of nature, one filled with "signs" that can be read by those possessed of intelligence in order to draw logical conclusions about the Divine and His purpose in creation. In the qur'ānic view, both kinds of *āyāt* are valid guides to and reminders of the Divine. The signs in nature, like the verses of the Revelation, are wondrous tokens of the nature and actions of God, His will for Creation, and His ability to fulfill His promise and threat to resurrect and judge all human beings in His good time. Natural phenomena are effectively the lenses through which the faithful – which is to say, the *fully human* beings, "those who are grateful" and show it in their responsiveness to God – can see the living presence of the Divine everywhere.

Graham thus sees the Qur'an in a broader perspective as a "discourse of signs" (2014, pp. 1, 8). Moreover, the above verses (Qur'an Dhāriyāt/51:20–21) also give people an important point to ponder and contemplate in the vast universe. This reflection will help, on the one hand, to explore nature as characterized by duality, that is, the world operates on the principle of pairs (*zawjayn*) (Qur'an Dhāriyāt/51:49), where complementary elements combine to create countless new forms and combinations in the universe, whereas, on the other hand, God is characterized by Unity (Baker, 1998, p. 98; Özdemir, 2003, p. 14). Not only this, numerous verses (including Qur'an Ṣaff/61:1; Qur'an Ḥajj/22:18; Qur'an Raḥmān/55:6) of the

Qur'an assert that all natural beings and phenomena have an awareness of Allah and glorify Him.

The Qur'an depicts God as *muḥīt* – all-encompassing. Whatever is in the universe is in His sight; thus, there is no way to hide from God. The Qur'an says: "Whatever is in the heavens and in the earth belongs to Allah; Allah encompasses everything" (Qur'an Nisā'/4: 126). The term *muḥīt* has also been interpreted as the environment (Nasr, 1998, p. 121). In "Islam and the Environmental Crisis" (1992), Nasr presents that "in reality, man is immersed in the Divine *Muḥīt* and is only unaware of it because of his forgetfulness and negligence (*ghaflah*), which is the underlying sin of the soul, only to be overcome by remembrance (*dhikr*)" (p. 89). Thus, to remember Allah is to see Him everywhere and to understand His reality as *Muḥīt*. As such, the Islamic perspective of nature and environment presents a multifaceted reality that enjoins human beings to use, read, respect, and love nature to realize the "Divine Presence of that Reality," which is our ultimate "environment" (Nasr, 1992, p. 89). Nasr's understanding of nature is close to both biocentrism and ecocentrism in that it views nature as having intrinsic value and thus warranting moral consideration.

The ultimate principle of "why nature exists and what it means" is worth noting. Ibrahim Özdemir, a Turkish professor of philosophy, tackles these key questions and argues that nature or the universe has a specific purpose, order, and wisdom that lead to the "existence of a Creator who is All-powerful, All-knowing, and All-Merciful" (Özdemir, 2003, p. 8). It suggests that the Qur'an aims to awaken humanity to a holistic understanding of its interactions with and relationship with God and the natural world. Several leading Muslim thinkers and commentators, such as Sa'īd Nūrsī (1878–1960), Mawlānā Abul Kalām Azād (1888–1958), and Sayyid Quṭb (1906–66), have paid special attention to demonstrate that nature is characterized by balance, harmony, and purpose (see Azad, 1971; Edis, 2008).

5.3 Principles of Environmental Ethics

Muslims believe that the Islamic ethical framework is based on a transcendental source of knowledge, Revelation (*waḥy*), which is regarded as the universally applicable source of knowledge. Muslim environmental ethicists and eco-Islamic writers have, thus, explored fundamental environmental or eco-ethical principles derived from the same revelation: the Qur'an.

The following is an explanation of the ethical principles that constitute the foundational framework of Islamic environmentalism. While all these principles are not universally defined, scholars may differ in their interpretation of them. However, certain principles, such as *tawḥīd* (unity), *khilāfah* (stewardship), and *ākhirah* (accountability), are considered fundamental. Without a proper understanding and description of these principles, along with other derived principles of *fiṭrah* (natural disposition) and *mizān* (balance), Islamic environmentalism would be incomplete.

5.3.1 Unity (Tawḥīd)

Tawḥīd is the overriding theme of the Qur'an; it is the cardinal belief and, hence, the essence of Islam. *Tawḥīd* refers to the belief in the absolute Oneness and Unity of Allah (God), the Creator, Sustainer, and Controller of all things. Nawal Ammar (2001, 2005, pp. 862–63) provides significant insights while explaining the *tawḥīd* and God–nature–human relationship concepts. She believes that *tawḥīd* must be understood at two different levels. In the first, *tawḥīd* declares the Oneness of God. For, the Qur'an says, "Say: He is Allah, the One and Unique. Allah, Who is in need of none and of Whom all are in need; He neither begot any nor was He begotten; and none is comparable to Him" (Qur'an Ikhlās/ 112:1–4). Similarly, the Qur'an explicitly says: "There is no God but He, the Creator of all things" (Qur'an An'ām/6:102). It exemplifies the recognition that there is one absolute, transcendent Creator of the universe and all it contains.

Tawḥīd holds profound implications for human behavior and thought, permeating various dimensions of personal and social life. This principle resonates within the realms of religion, ethics, politics, social dynamics, epistemology, and scientific pursuits, shaping the very fabric of Islamic thought and practice. *Tawḥīd* encompasses the episteme of monotheism and its application to diverse world systems and their interrelations. It recognizes the interconnectedness between the unity of God and the laws governing the universe.

The world witnessed remarkable scientific development during the golden age of Muslim civilization (eighth to thirteenth century). Arguably, *tawḥīd* played a central role in this regard as it guided people with rational inquiry about the natural world. *Tawḥīd* emphasized the unity of knowledge and encouraged Muslims to seek understanding in various domains, including scientific exploration. Islamic scholars during that time viewed scientific inquiry as a means to deepen their understanding of God's creation and uncover the wisdom and order embedded within it. This perspective fostered a conducive environment for scientific progress. Scholarly studies (Campanini, 2015) recognize the diverse and complex nature of scientific contributions during early Islamic civilization, but an argument suggests that the Islamic perspective on the universe created a conducive environment, influencing scientists from diverse religious backgrounds and contributing to a distinctive era of progress not seen in earlier times.

Consequently, *tawḥīd* is at the heart of Muslim curiosity about the nature of the universe (Sardar, 1985, p. 225, 2006, pp. 97–98; Khalid, 2002, p. 338; Saniotis, 2012, p. 157). The absolute Oneness of God shapes Muslim understanding of nature or the universe. The Tawhidic worldview links nature with the divine but does not make it sacred in and of itself. To consider any creation as sacred is to associate something or someone with Allah, and that is the opposite of *tawḥīd* or the oneness of Allah (see Qur'an Ḥā Mīm/41:6; Qur'an Nisā'/4:36; Qur'an Luqmān/31:13; Qur'an Nisā'/4:48; Qur'an Fātiḥah/1:5; Qur'an Baqarah/2:22; Qur'an Isrā'/17:23).

Islam categorically opposes the notions of "nature as God" (pantheism) and "God in nature." That does not mean, however, that nature is secular or profane; it is respected and valued in that it reflects the Will and fulfills the purpose of God (Ammar, 2001, p. 196, 2005, p. 862). On many occasions, the Qur'an reveals nature as: "To Him belongs all that is in the heavens and all that is in the earth, and all that is in between, and all that is beneath the soil" (Ṭāḥā, 20:6). And since on many occasions (see Qur'an Qāf/50:6–8; Qur'an Anbiyā'/21:30; Qur'an Ra'd/13:2; Qur'an Nisā'/4:126; Qur'an An'ām/6:73) the Qur'an speaks of nature praising God's glory, power, and might. One verse clearly says, "To Him belong all who are in the heavens and all who are on the earth. All are in obedience to Him" (Qur'an Rūm/30:26), and as such, nature should be respected and protected, not because it is sacred, but because it reflects God's Unity. This unity in creation, as Ammar emphasises, is the second level of *tawḥīd* (Ammar, 2005, p. 863).

This perspective creates the duality of the Creator and the created, which renders the latter in Islam (e.g., nature, humans, animals, plants, and other creatures) equal and alike – "a unified class of God's creation" (Lubis, 1998; Ammar, 2001, p. 196). Moreover, Ammar further explains that the tawhidic viewpoint guides to three key points in understanding the relationship between God and His creation: "everything on earth is created by God, everything that God creates reflects His sacredness, and that everything on earth worships the same God" (Ammar, 2001, pp. 193–194). Hence, *tawḥīd* reflects the unity and interconnectedness of nature or natural order as an important and distinctive principle of ecology and environmental science (Kamali, 2016, p. 175).

Tawḥīd also emphasizes that a comprehension of the metaphysical aspects of the Creator has profound ethical ramifications, as humans are obligated to act morally in obedience to Him and fulfill His commands. The universe operates as an integrated and interconnected system, where various components work together in harmony and balance. This functioning unity reflects the doctrinal concept of the Oneness of God. Any disharmony, imbalance, or breach created in nature would directly affect our relationship with the Creator. In other words,

God directs us to behave with nature so as not to cause any disorder or corruption on the Earth. Instead, become the guardians on the Earth while extracting benefits from nature. As a result, from *tawḥīd* emerge the concepts of *khilāfah* and *amānah* – which set out the purpose and nature of human conduct on the Earth.

*5.3.2 Stewardship (*Khilāfah*)*

Though there is interdependence and equality among the creatures of God, humans have a unique role and responsibility. The Qur'an says, "I am about to place a vicegerent on earth" (Qur'an Baqarah/2:30) and "it is Who has appointed you vicegerent over the earth" (Qur'an An'ām/6: 165). These verses provide essential insights about humans' place and position in this universe compared to other creatures. Islam thus entrusts all the affairs of the Earth to humans as the *khalīfah* (vicegerents) or custodians of the Earth. There are other interpretations of *khalīfah* (Foltz, 2013, p. 670), yet this term has generally been understood as referring to human vicegerency, trusteeship, or '*khilāfah*' on the Earth. However, *khilāfah* implies comparatively a greater sense of moral responsibility to look after the considerable panorama of God's creation.

A *khalīfah* must hold trust in following God's will. According to Muslim environmental ethicists (Zaman, 1986; Bagader, 1994), this principle implies, by virtue of specific authority and qualities (see Qur'an Baqarah/2:28; Qur'an Tīn/95:4; and Qur'an Ṣād/38:72), that God grants humans, individually and collectively, the role of trustees or stewards. They are entrusted with treasures to enjoy within restrictions: to manage them, to harness them, to improve and better them, and to preserve them for sustainable use. Any misuse and abuse of bounties from God is vehemently disliked and prohibited in Islam.

In sum, humans should consider themselves vicegerents, not dictatorial lords and masters of the planet. This has enormous environmental ramifications. Vicegerency or *khilāfah* is further guided by the principles of trusteeship (*amānah*), which embody a principle of accountability (*ākhirah*).

*5.3.3 Trusteeship (*Amānah*) and Accountability (*Ākhirah*)*

In the context of the concept of *khilāfah*, a related concept is *amānah* or trust. *Amānah* is interpreted in various ways by different scholars: some see it as embodying the notion of "religious obligation," that is, the rights and duties toward both God and humanity (Kathīr, 1999, pp. 488–489); some understand it as referring to human reason and free will. The "trust" was accepted by humans when all other creatures refused it. Within the realm of Islamic environmental ethics, there is a broader understanding of "*amānah*" that extends to encompass the entire universe, emphasizing the inherent responsibilities that humans hold toward the natural world (Ouis, 1998, p. 158). As stated in the Qur'an, God proclaimed: "We offered the trust to the heavens and the earth and the mountains, but they refused to carry it and were afraid of doing so; but man carried it. Surely he is wrong-doing, ignorant" (Qur'an Aḥzāb/33: 72). Thus, God entrusted humans with this sacred obligation, which they accepted through a transcendent covenant between themselves and God. Consequently, humans have the capacity to live a life of righteousness or engage in wrongdoing since they possess the reasoning ability to discern between right and wrong. According to Setia (2007), the term "*amānah*" is intimately connected to the concept of "*amn*" (security), encompassing both "its physical and spiritual dimensions" (p. 130).

However, humanity's elevated status comes with a heavy moral burden. Humans are superior not because they have more power, control, or authority than other creatures, but because they are accountable to Allah. Accountability stems from the trust or *amānah* they have accepted (Haq, 2001b, p. 150).

This responsibility and accountability thus demand humans adhere to the best moral conduct and display the highest ethical principles. This ethical paradigm includes all generations, together with all other forms of life in the universe, emphasizing humans' responsibility to all living beings. It is therefore incumbent upon humanity to make prudent use of the natural resources they have been given by applying the wisdom, insight, and knowledge they have been endowed with (Mohamed, 2017). As part of their devotional obligations, Muslims are entrusted with caring for God's creation, and "they will be held accountable" on the Day of Judgment (*ākhirah*) if they fail to do so (Ammar, 2005). This moral imperative instils in the adherents of Islam an essential component of activism that, if fully internalized, has far-reaching positive implications for ecological conservation. The principle of accountability determines a test for Muslims and is central to framing a pragmatic ethical system (Wersal, 1995, p. 452).

God's grace, like His sovereignty, extends beyond the riches of the natural world in this life to His final kindness for the faithful on the Last Day. Here, too, nature is used as proof of what God has promised in scripture: that all the dead will be resurrected, judgment will occur, God will be gracious to penitent sinners if they are loyal, and the righteous will inherit paradise forever (Graham, 2016, pp. 120–122). Many verses of the Qur'an confirm that life is but a test (see Qur'an Baqarah/2, 155; Qur'an Muhammad/47:31). One of the most eloquent statements of this is found in Sūrah Mulk (67:2): "Who created death and life that He might try you as to which of you is better in deed"; on another occasion, the Qur'an speaks, "We shall subject you to ill and good by way of trial" (Qur'an Anbiyā'/21:35; see also Qur'an Hūd/11:7 and Qur'an

Kahf/18:7). This is further supported by a portion of a *ḥadīth*, where Abū Saʿīd Khudrī reported that the Prophet Muhammad said, "The world is sweet and green (alluring), and verily Allah is going to install you as vicegerent in it in order to see how you act" (Muslim, *Ṣaḥīḥ Muslim*, Book 49, Ḥadīth 99, 2007, p. 112); in another *ḥadīth*, the Prophet Muhammad stated: "Each of you is a shepherd and will be answerable for those under his care" (Al-Bukhārī, *Ṣaḥīḥ al-Bukhārī*, Book 67, Ḥadīth 5182, 1997, p. 81).

Consequently, in Islam, humans have a dual relationship with nature. On the one hand, they are custodians of nature, yet they are also its users. Many verses of the Qur'an eloquently utter: "Have you not seen that Allah has subjected to your service all that is in the heavens and on the earth and has abundantly bestowed upon you all His bounties, both visible and invisible?" (Qur'an Luqmān/31:20); "He it is Who made the earth subservient to you. So traverse in its tracks and partake of the sustenance He has provided" (Qur'an Mulk/67:15); "He has subjected for you the night and the day and the sun and the moon and the stars have also been made subservient by His command. . . . And He it is Who has subjected the sea that you may eat fresh fish from it and bring forth ornaments from it that you can wear. And you see ships ploughing their course through it so that you may go forth seeking His Bounty and be grateful to Him" (Qur'an Naḥl/16:12–14).

This dual role of *khalīfah* as trustee and user of the Earth is "unique in rights as well as in responsibilities" (Kula, 2001) and summarizes the Islamic ecological ethic (Zaidi, 1981 and Dutton, 1998). Gade (2019, p. 154) emphasizes the impact of unseen factors on human actions; religion connects the unseen, such as the fate of the deceased, to environmental justice, providing practical implications for this world.

*5.3.4 Natural Disposition (*Fiṭrah*)*

The principle of *fiṭrah* in Islam reflects living in a natural and inherent state of order, forming an integral part of the religion known as *dīn al-fiṭrah* (Chishti, 2003, pp. 67, 77–79; Khalid, 2003, p. 315). It describes an original natural state, pattern, or pure state into which humankind and all other creatures were brought into being, which is "*by nature* submissive (*muslim*) to God" (Graham, 2016, p. 123). Embedded in this original natural pattern operate divine norms or *Sunnah Allah* (Qur'an Aḥzāb/33: 64), which serve as unchanging principles that shape the world, while human behavior determines the distinction between good and evil. These actions have consequences, not only in the afterlife but also in the present world. Therefore, any imbalance or interference leads to malfunctioning in humans and the nature of which they are an integral part. In order to express the inherent nature of humanity within the universe, individuals must acknowledge their innate disposition and the structured harmony upon which the cosmos is founded.

The key verse of the Qur'an in which *fiṭrah* occurs tells us: "[T]urn your face to the true Faith and adhere to the true nature on which Allah has created human beings. The mould fashioned by Allah cannot be altered. That is the True, Straight Faith, although most people do not know" (Qur'an Rūm/30:30). This is supported by several statements by the Prophet Muhammad, including "Every child born is born in a state of *fiṭrah*" (Al-Bukhārī, *Ṣaḥīḥ al-Bukhārī*, Book 23, Ḥadīth 1385, 1997, p. 267). The Qur'anic verse (Qur'an Rūm/30:30), therefore, taken together with other verses that speak of Allah's creation (e.g. Qur'an Raḥmān/55:3-5), provides deep insights into the eco-ethic of Islam (Khalid, 1998, pp. 21–31, 2003, p. 315, 2007, pp. 131–133). Therefore, individuals are admonished against disrupting or altering this inherent, primordial, unchanging pattern of the natural disposition of humanity and the universe, which displays harmony, equilibrium, and interconnectedness.

*5.3.5 Balance (*Mīzān*)*

The universe embodies a system of well-knit design, characterized by a harmonious and balanced arrangement, and a flawless order where everything is precisely measured. Numerous verses of the Qur'an emphasize that this universe is defined by a dynamic and perfect equilibrium or balance (*mīzān*) often referred to as "the principle of *mīzān*" (Khalid, 2005, p. 881). *Mīzān* is an overarching principle: it signifies that there exists a balance among different but interconnected components of the natural environment (Ouis, 1998, p. 162; Agwan, 2000; Haq, 2001b, p. 153). The natural world's innate disposition to submit to the Will of its creator, God, is seen as the source of such a balance.

The Qur'an says: "The sun and the moon follow a reckoning, and the stars and the trees all prostrate themselves, and He has raised up the heaven and has set a balance that you may not transgress in the balance, but weigh things equitably and skimp not in the balance. And He has set up the earth for all beings" (Qur'an Raḥmān/55:5–10). On other occasions, the Qur'an clearly states: "Who created the seven heavens one upon another. You will see no incongruity in the Merciful One's creation. Turn your vision again, can you see any flaw?" (Qur'an Mulk/76:3). Similarly, the Qur'an speaks: "As for the earth, We have stretched it out and have cast on it firm mountains, and have caused to grow in it everything well-measured" (Qur'an Ḥijr/15:19).

What it brings is that God speaks in the Qur'an about a delicate equilibrium in which everything has been placed. This is significant because the balance underlies God's wisdom, purpose, and power in the creation, as mentioned in Section 5.2. So, nature should be a source of inspiration and thought for "understanding the divine operation in creation" (Saniotis, 2012, p. 157), which is also a form of worship (Matin, 2010, p. 12).

The *mīzān* thus provides critical insights as guidelines for restoring the lost environmental balance. While giving a broader explanation of the principle of *fiṭrah*, Khalid (1992, p. 103) says: "We have lost the art of living in the *fiṭrah* state that is the natural state, in balance and harmony with creation." The teachings of the Qur'an and the Prophetic traditions consistently emphasize the importance of maintaining balance in human behavior and the responsible use of resources. These sources instruct individuals to avoid wastefulness, excess, and actions that disrupt (*fasād*) the established order in Creation, causing harm or destruction. The following explanation delves into further detail on this principle of balance and its significance.

5.4 Other Islamic Ethical Teachings

The Islamic notion of environment protection, as eco-Islamic writers assert, is further guided by two significant Islamic teachings: *al-ma'rūf* (good) and *al-munkar* (evil) (Ammar, 2001, p. 201). On several occasions, the Qur'an enjoins Muslims: "And from among you there must be a party who invite people to all that is good and enjoin the doing of all that is right and forbid the doing of all that is wrong" (Qur'an 'Imrān/3:104). This maxim implies practical constraints, which, if not adhered to, invites punishment in the hereafter. Scholars (e.g., Sardar, 2006) extend its scope to include the environment, viewing it through the lens of *ḥalāl* (that which is approved) and *ḥarām* (that which is prohibited). On a closer look, all human actions harmful to society or the environment are strongly prohibited in Islam. Similarly, people's actions that are beneficial to society or the environment are allowed and appreciated.

*5.4.1 Corruption and Mischief-Making on the Earth (*Fasād fī al-Arḍ*)*

Fasād is a central concept in eco-Islamic thought. *Fasād*, which means "destruction," "corruption," or "mischief," is often believed to extend to the environmental sphere as well (Ammar, 2001; Haq, 2003; Setia, 2007). It is the consequence of transgressing or violating God-ordained restrictions on human behavior. It is worth noting and significant that the scope of "*Fasād*" as elucidated in the Qur'an encompasses a multitude of mischiefs and disorders. These include acts of corruption, injustice, oppression, violence, deceit, dishonesty, exploitation, and other behaviors that disrupt the equilibrium and harmony of individuals and society. The Qur'an serves as a moral guide, urging individuals to uphold righteousness, justice, and ethical conduct, while cautioning against any actions that undermine the natural order and social cohesion. As such, the corruption inflicted by humankind in the form of environmental pollution and an ecological crisis is seen as the direct outcome of human behavioral or spiritual crisis, which resulted in his interference with and wrong approach to the natural environment. The Qur'an says: "Evil has become rife on the land and at sea because of men's deeds" (Qur'an Rūm/30:41). Thus, to maintain the goodness on the Earth, to improve the harmony in the environment, and to balance the use and protection of natural resources, Islamic environmental ethicists assert that it is imperative to heed the divine admonitions. The consequences of making mischief on the Earth are clearly mentioned in numerous verses of the Qur'an: "Surely We destroyed the nations (which had risen to heights of glory in their times) before you when they indulged in wrong doing" (Qur'an Yūnus/10: 13); "Whenever he attains authority, he goes about the earth spreading mischief and laying to waste crops and human life, even though Allah (whose testimony he invokes) does not love mischief" (Qur'an Baqarah/2: 205). God explicitly warns people to "make no mischief on the earth after it has been set in good order" (Qur'an A'rāf/7:56, 85). In other words, because humans have destroyed the natural order, humankind is on the verge of annihilation by the forces of nature.

*5.4.2 Extravagance and Waste (*Isrāf *and* Tabdhīr*)*

As mentioned in Section 5.4.1, the Qur'an defines various forms of mischief and harm that can result from imbalanced behavior and unethical actions. The Qur'an warns against disrupting the established order of creation. This includes avoiding actions that lead to the destruction of crops (Qur'an Baqarah/2: 205), dishonesty in measurements and payments, economic disparities, encroachment on the rights of others (Qur'an A'rāf/7: 85; Qur'an Shūrā/26: 183), disruption of a just system (Qur'an Naml/27: 34), and committing crimes or corruption (Qur'an Yūsuf/12: 73).

In the Qur'an, specific references can be found regarding the consequences of wastefulness (*tabdhīr*) and extravagance (*isrāf*) in verses such as Qur'an A'rāf (7:31) and Qur'an Shūrā (26:151–152). In Surah Isrā' (17:26–27), individuals who partake in wasteful and extravagant behaviors are referred to as the "Brothers of Satan." These verses highlight the spiritual and moral repercussions associated with such actions, emphasizing their negative impact.

It is noteworthy that Muslim scholars, including Muhammed Al-Jurjānī (1339–1414), have drawn a technical distinction between the two terms. Al-Jurjānī explains that extravagance involves spending wealth in a permissible manner but in excessive amounts, while wastefulness refers to spending wealth in impermissible ways (Al-Jurjānī, 1985, p. 26). This distinction provides further clarity and understanding of the concepts of wastefulness and extravagance as described in Islamic scholarship. Overall, it highlights their relevance to issues of overconsumption and excessive consumerism as prevalent in the contemporary world. According to the Qur'an, engaging in wastefulness and extravagance is morally corrupt and driven by evil. Taking care of these concepts has a direct impact on an individual's spirituality. What is interesting here is that these concepts implicitly promote the idea of sustainable use of resources. For our discussion, it leads to the adoption of the principle of 3 R's – Reduce, Recycle, and Reuse – which has far-reaching implications for the mitigation of the contemporary environmental crisis.

Animal waste has been utilized as a valuable resource since ancient times. In the context of biomass, it can be processed and converted into biogas, thereby serving as a renewable source of energy. Islamic *fiqh* literature provides detailed discussions on the utilization of animal excrement and other waste products (Ministry of Awqaf, 2005, p. 204), offering guidelines aligned with Islamic ethical and legal principles. By raising public awareness about the permissible use of animal waste in accordance with Islamic teachings, a comprehensive approach can be adopted. Furthermore, adopting various scientific methods becomes essential for harnessing energy from animal waste, producing organic manure, implementing water storage techniques, and employing other scientific approaches in a prudent manner. By integrating an ethical, legal, and scientific framework, a three-tiered approach can be employed to explore and implement sustainable practices in energy, natural resource management, and environmental preservation. By aligning with sustainable behavior, we can effectively address the scope of wastefulness and extravagance.

People who are wasteful and extravagant are damaging society and abdicating their human responsibilities toward society and the environment. Although Islam allows taking legitimate advantage of divine bounty (*ni'mah*), any waste or excess is strongly forbidden in Islam and leads to punishment.

*5.4.3 Beauty and Cleanliness (*Jamāl and Ṭahārah*)*

On digging deeper into the Islamic ethical teachings, one finds that a significant feature reflected in the universe is divine "aesthetics" or "beauty" (*jamāl*). This feature seeks to attract human attention to divine beauty, for it is "equated with recognition of truth and perfection" (Haider, 1984, p. 179). The beauty found in Creation (Qur'an Naḥl/16:6, 8; Qur'an Luqmān/ 31:10; Qur'an Ghāfir/40:64; Qur'an Qāf/50:7-8) – on land, at sea, and in the heavens – confirms both God's beauty and His power. Elsewhere, the Qur'an emphasizes the divine beauty of

His names and attributes (Qur'an A'rāf/7:180). Significant to this teaching, the Prophet Muhammad is reported to have said, "Allah is beautiful and He loves beauty" (Muslim, *Ṣaḥīḥ Muslim*, Book 1, Ḥadīth 147, 2007, p. 178). It implies that faith in God's beauty should encourage individuals to care about the beauty of their words and actions, particularly their concern with the environment as much as their physical appearance. Moreover, God's bounties for humans are *ṭayyib* and *ṭāhir* (good, pure, and clean), for, like *jamāl*, God also favors cleanliness and purity (Qur'an Baqarah/2:222). Often, scholars fail to recognize that beauty and cleanliness have Islamic values for environmental preservation. The Prophet emphasizes cleanliness as an essential habit of the Muslim's everyday life, because people's health and efficiency depend on a clean and healthy environment. He said: "Cleanliness is half of faith" (Muslim, *Ṣaḥīḥ Muslim*, Book 2, Ḥadīth 1, 2007, p. 354).

Both the concepts of *jamāl* (beauty) and *ṭahārah* (cleanliness) hold significant implications for addressing environmental degradation, particularly in relation to air pollution and public hygiene (Brimblecombe, 1993, p. 78). *Jamāl* focuses on the preservation and enhancement of natural beauty within the environment, emphasizing the importance of maintaining clean air, pristine landscapes, and aesthetically pleasing surroundings.

Likewise, *ṭahārah* emphasizes cleanliness and hygiene, both at an individual and communal level. This encompasses proper waste management, the maintenance of clean water sources, and the establishment of sanitary conditions in public spaces. These were common practices employed during medieval Muslim civilization as discussed earlier. By promoting cleanliness and hygiene, *ṭahārah* contributes to the prevention of environmental pollution and the spread of diseases.

Moreover, *jamāl* and *ṭahārah* align with Islamic principles of stewardship (*khilāfah*) and the responsibility to care for the environment. By cultivating an appreciation for natural beauty and prioritizing cleanliness, these concepts encourage individuals and communities to adopt sustainable practices that minimize environmental degradation and safeguard public health.

Jamāl and *ṭahārah* also hold significant implications for addressing climate change. Embracing cleaner behaviors in individuals' lives can foster a heightened awareness of controlling air pollution at both individual and community levels. As highlighted earlier, Islamic tradition strongly condemns the pollution of land, air, and water. In light of the recognition that maintaining a clean environment is an act of worship, Islamic teachings can serve as a catalyst for changing toward renewable energy sources and adopting eco-friendly practices that minimize the impact on climate change. Considering the current pace and relentless pursuit of economic development, achieving these goals may pose challenges. Nonetheless, it is crucial to acknowledge that while difficult, it is not impossible to align economic progress with sustainable practices.

5.4.4 Attitude toward Animals and Plants

In Islam, believers are constantly aware of the reality that their "Lord is the one who has given everything its form and guided it" (Qur'an Ṭāhā/20:50). This understanding underscores the recognition that all things, including living beings, have been shaped and guided by the divine. The Qur'an emphasizes that, like human beings as a community, God also created communities among animals and plants. In Surah *al-An'ām*, He says, "There is no animal that crawls on the earth, no bird that flies with its two wings, but are communities like you" (Qur'an An'ām/6:38). Not only that explicit references to animals and plants abound in the Qur'an. Six chapters of the Qur'an bear animal names: the cow (2), the cattle (6), the bee (16), the ant (28), the spider (29), and the elephant (105). To get a clear understanding of Islam's concern with nonhuman beings, it is necessary to know Islam's attitude toward the animal and plant kingdoms.

The Prophet Muhammad demonstrated a deep concern, care, and love for the kind treatment of animals, extending even to their slaughter. He explicitly prohibited any form of harm or cruelty toward animals and emphasized the need to protect their rights. These teachings reflect a compassionate approach toward animals and serve as a reminder of the ethical responsibility humans have toward the animal kingdom. Based on numerous *ḥadīths*, the Prophet Muhammad is seen developing a spirit of love and care toward nonhumans. He forbade any sort of ill-treatment of them, for instance beating and branding of animals on face (Al-Bukhārī, *Ṣaḥīḥ al-Bukhārī*, Book 72, Ḥadīth 5541, 1997, p. 263), conscientious slaughtering (Muslim, *Ṣaḥīḥ Muslim*, Book 34, Ḥadīth 57, 2007, p. 293), killing them for sport and entertainment (Al-Bukhārī, *Ṣaḥīḥ al-Bukhārī*, Book 72, Ḥadīth 5514, 1997, p. 254), cutting parts off while it is alive (Al-Bukhārī, *Ṣaḥīḥ al-Bukhārī*, Book 72, Ḥadīth 5515, 1997, p. 255; Al-Nasā'ī, *Sunan Al-Nasā'ī*, Book 43, Ḥadīth 4447, 2007, p. 249), and making animals fight each other (Al-Tirmidhī, *Jāmi' Al-Tirmidhī*, Book 21, Ḥadīth 1708, 2007, p. 442). It is an obligation to feed an animal and to take care of it if it is ill. The Prophet Muhammad said: "A woman was tormented because of a cat which she had kept locked up until it died, and she was thrown into Hell for that. She neither gave it food or drink when she locked it up nor freed it so that it would eat from the vermin of the earth" (Al-Bukhārī, *Ṣaḥīḥ al-Bukhārī*, Book 42, Ḥadīth 2365, 1997, p. 318; Muslim, *Ṣaḥīḥ Muslim*, Book 39, Hadith 2243, 2007, p. 101). Even when the Prophet Muhammad was asked, "Is there a reward doing good with these animals"? He said, "There is a reward in doing good to every living thing" (Al-Bukhārī, *Ṣaḥīḥ al-Bukhārī*, Book 46, Ḥadīth 2466, 1997, pp. 273–273). This is further confirmed in another *ḥadīth* where God forgives a sinner after she waters a dog dying of thirst (Al-Bukhārī, *Ṣaḥīḥ al-Bukhārī*, Book 59, Ḥadīth 3321, 1997, p. 322).

In addition, the Prophet Muhammad also stated: "Whoever kills a sparrow or anything bigger than that without a just cause, God will hold him accountable on the Day of Judgment" (Al-Nasā'ī, *Sunan Al-Nasā'ī*, Book 43, Ḥadīth 4450, 2007, p. 250); he prohibited the killing of certain animals, such as ants, bees, hoopoes, and sparrow-hawks (Dāwūd, *Sunan Abū Dāwūd*, Book 42, Ḥadīth 5267, 2008, p. 485). Therefore, Islam not only condemns to hell those who mistreat animals but also bestows extraordinary grace upon those who show them kindness (Foltz, 2006a, p. 152). Furthermore, within Islamic law, the discussion of animal rights becomes inevitable when considering conservation efforts. The notion of rights being restored to their rightful owners on the Day of Resurrection is expressed in the Prophetic tradition: "Rights will certainly be restored to those entitled to them on the Day of Resurrection, to the point that even the hornless sheep will lay claim upon the horned one" (Muslim, *Ṣaḥīḥ Muslim*, Book 45, Ḥadīth 60, 2007, pp. 447–448). This tradition highlights the profound concept of justice and the equitable recompense that awaits individuals in the afterlife. According to Llewellyn (2002, p. 233), "the rights of animals, *huqūq al-bahā'im wa 'l-hayawān*, are enshrined as one of the categories of *huqūq al-'ibād*, the rights of God's servants, that is, human beings and animals."

Numerous *ḥadīths* explicitly speak of the value of plants and trees. For example, "[h]e who cuts a lote tree [without justification], God will send him to Hellfire" (Dāwūd, *Sunan Abū Dāwūd*, Book 43, Ḥadīth 5239, 2008, pp. 473–474). And, "[i]f any Muslim plants a tree or sows a field, and a human, bird or animal eats from it, it shall be reckoned as charity from him" (Al-Bukhārī, *Ṣaḥīḥ al-Bukhārī*, Book 41, Ḥadīth 2320, 1997, pp. 293; Al-Tirmidhī, *Jami'Al-Tirmidhī*, Book 13, Ḥadīth 1382, 2007, p. 173). The Prophet displayed so much respect for plants and trees that he said, "[i]f the day of resurrection comes upon anyone of you while he has a seedling in hand, let him plant it" (Ahmad, *Musnad Ahmad*, Book 32, Ḥadīth 2902, 2001, p. 251).

These examples demonstrate that Islamic sources are abundant in terms of the status and attitude toward nonhuman beings, such that caring for them earns reward and cruel or ill-treatment earns punishment. Care for the environment, as exemplified by the Prophet Muhammad, was continued by his successors, and followed by others throughout Islamic history (Ammar, 2001, p. 202). The first caliph of Islam, Abū Bakr, provided specific instructions to the departing army to Syria led by Uthāma, which included environmental considerations. He emphasized the prohibition of uprooting or burning date palms, cutting down fruit-bearing trees, or slaughtering animals unless it was for consumption purposes. These instructions demonstrate a concern for environmental preservation and the responsible use of natural resources (Al-Ṭabarī, 1967 p. 227). Bringing dead land back to life through cultivation and plantation, as well as protecting the plant kingdom, are both valuable and rewarding services to humanity. However, the present scenario reminds us how much has been lost, as Muslims often do not abide by these regulations.

5.4.5 Respect for Water

Water is a blessing from God and is essential to life. The Qur'an sees it as the source of life and one of the most precious commodities essential to all: human, animal, and plant. The Qur'an emphasizes: "We made every living being out of water" (Qur'an An'ām/21:30); and "in the water which Allah sends down from the sky and thereby quickens the earth after it was dead" (Qur'an Baqarah/2:164). There are numerous occasions in the Qur'an where God speaks of the importance of water. The Qur'an contains indirect directives emphasizing the importance of regulating water and waterways, treating them as shared resources. It says: "Let them know that the water should be divided between them and the she-camel, each availing their turn" (Qur'an Qamar/54:28).

The Qur'an does not provide specific guidelines on the utilization of natural resources. However, Islamic Law and the Sunnah offer valuable insights in this regard. A *ḥadīth* of the Prophet Muhammad sheds light on the importance of distributing natural resources in a socially beneficial manner. He stated: "People are partners in three things: water, fire, and pastures" (Dāwūd, *Sunan Abū Dāwūd*, Book 23, Ḥadīth 3477, 2008, pp. 129–130). This *ḥadīth* implies the significance of equitable distribution and responsible management of natural resources for the collective well-being of society.

Similar environmental concerns for water in many traditions of the Prophet Muhammad are even more striking. Excessive use, overconsumption, wastage, impairment, pollution, and destruction of water are seen as detestable and prohibited. Apart from being a necessity of life, water also has socioreligious importance in Islam. The Prophet Muhammad forbade his followers from wasting water, even when it was in plenty or being used for religious purposes (Mājah, *Sunan Ibn Mājah*, Book 1, Ḥadīth 424, 2007, p. 324). The Prophet's approach and care for water aimed to discourage wasteful attitudes toward nature's gifts (Bagader *et al.*, 1994; Kula, 2001). A frequently cited *ḥadīth* in Islamic environmental literature concerns water consumption: "The Messenger of Allah passed by Sa'd when he was performing ablution, and he said: 'What is this extravagance?' He said, 'Can there be any extravagance in ablution?' He said: 'Yes, even if you are on the bank of a flowing river'" (Mājah, *Sunan Ibn Mājah*, Book 1, Ḥadīth 425, 2007, p. 324). Similarly, polluting and contaminating water is forbidden. The Prophet Muhammad is said to have "prohibited urinating in stagnant water" (Muslim, *Ṣaḥīḥ Muslim*, Book 2, Ḥadīth 94, 2007, p. 405); another narration says, "Be on your guard against three things that provoke cursing: easing in the watering places, on the thoroughfares, and in the shade (of the tree)" (Dāwūd, *Sunan Abū Dāwūd*, Book 1, Ḥadīth 26, 2008, p. 40).

Based on these examples, wastage and contamination of water is strongly prohibited in Islam. The ethics of water use in Islam is connected to Muslim faith, behavior, and responsibility, guided by Islamic teachings and regulations enshrined in Islamic *Sharī'ah*. The aforementioned traditions clearly indicate Islam's stance on the conservation and judicious use of natural resources, particularly water. That wastage or excessive water use is vividly detestable, even in circumstances where the loss or misuse of water may seem inconceivable.

Drawing upon the aforementioned *ḥadīth* (Mājah, *Sunan Ibn Mājah*, Book 1, Ḥadīth 425, 2007, p. 324), Özdemir (2003, p. 9) poses a thought-provoking question: To what extent does the Islamic prohibition against extravagance and wastefulness hold even in situations where circumstances do not necessitate such actions? By contemplating this reflection, one recognizes the broader implications of Islamic teachings, advocating for a balanced and measured approach in various spheres.

5.5 Concluding Thoughts on Islam and Environmental Ethics

In sum, Islamic environmental ethics stresses the unity in creation, and reminds humans of their duty as stewards (*khalīfah*) to exercise their power in maintaining equilibrium and fulfilling their responsibilities toward the Earth. It advocates for maintaining balance, harmony, and environmental preservation, and emphasizes the need for responsible environmental practices, acknowledging that human dominance over nature is temporary and subject to ethical constraints.

6 Practical Muslim Approaches to Contemporary Environmental Ethics

In certain Muslim societies, the implementation of Islamic environmentalism or eco-theology, in collaboration with governmental institutions, has demonstrated noteworthy efficacy in mitigating environmental degradation. Presented next are a few notable practical instances exemplifying the successful implementation of Islamic environmental ethics.

6.1 *Re-thinking the Unthinkable*: IFEES and the Case of Zanzibar

Fazlun Khalid's IFEES is one of the most active organizations in many Muslim countries. In 1999, IFEES was called in by an international agency to Zanzibar (Tanzania), where the Muslim fishermen were implementing blast fishing techniques (using explosives) to increase the fish catch, which was illegal and threatening to the ecosystem. Despite government regulations and charities, blast fishing continued unabated. Only through the efforts of IFEES was a two-day Qur'an workshop offered. Lacking explicit guidance regarding the use of explosives for catching fish in Islamic scripture, IFEES employed juristic reasoning (*Ijtihād*, i.e., Jurist's utmost effort within their capabilities to arrive at a considered opinion with respect to a legal judgment) to conclude that such practice is prohibited in Islam. As a result, blast fishing was largely abandoned in Zanzibar (Johnston, 2012, p. 230; Amirpur, 2021, p. 49).

Notably, IFEES published *Muslim Green Guide to Reducing Climate Change* in 2008, which became an important text and practical guidebook for Muslims to engage with the environment. It is a practical handbook that provides Islamic perspectives on various aspects of daily life within households, offering effective strategies to address climate change. It offers insights and recommendations for bringing about transformations in key aspects, including food, water, laundry, heating, electricity, transport, and recycling. The guide serves as a resource for individuals seeking practical ways to make a positive impact on climate change from an Islamic perspective. The IFEES plays a significant role in raising awareness and mobilizing the Muslim community globally to adopt a more environment-friendly lifestyle. Through literature targeting both adults and school-age children, they aim to educate and encourage individuals to choose greener practices while urging governments to address climate change and biodiversity loss (Johnston, 2012, p. 229).

6.2 Mobilizing *Fatāwā* (Legal Opinions) in Indonesia and Egypt

Indonesia, the world's most populous Muslim country, has attracted significant attention in terms of Islamic environmental activism in recent years. Environmental experts, Islamic organizations, and government agencies are working together to demonstrate environmental efforts in response to climate change. The three largest Islamic organizations in Indonesia that are actively engaged in environmental efforts are *Majlis Ulamā' Indonesia* (MUI), or the Indonesian Council of Islamic Scholars; *Nahdatul Ulamā'* (NU); and *Muhammadiyah*.

MUI, which is a national organization and was established by the state in 1975, issues *fatāwā* (juristic opinions) concerning the environment. International agencies frequently seek the MUI to carry out Islamic environmental messages. MUI has issued several significant *fatāwā* since 2010, which have been lauded by the global media for their implications. For instance, in 2014, a *fatwā*, informally called the "tiger fatwa," was issued against wildlife trafficking of endangered species, which reflect the best example of Islamic concern for wildlife protection. Similarly, in 2016, a *fatwā* was issued against the practise of open burning of forests and declared unauthorized deforestation "sinful" and "prohibited" (*ḥarām*), and the villagers complied. Earlier in 2010, similar rulings were issued for "environmentally friendly mining."

Other Indonesian organizations (NU and *Muhammadiyah*) have also been engaged locally in activities such as plantation, recycling of wastewater, and waste management (see Gade, 2019, pp. 145–154; Jamil, 2022). There are other success stories of environmental activism among Indonesian "Ulamā" – Muslim scholars with expertise in Islamic law and theology. The efforts of these organizations and the impact of religious legal rulings have been successful in social mobilization to realize social and environmental justice in Indonesia.

Similarly, ahead of COP27 (Conference of the Parties to the United Nations Framework Convention on Climate Change), which was held in Egypt in November 2022, the 7th International Conference of Fatwa Authorities Worldwide took place, which was organized by Egypt's Dār al-Iftā' (Islamic advisory and justiciary body). This conference brought together scholars and legal experts from ninety countries along with the representatives from the United Nations and the World Health Organization. During the event, a "Fatwa Charter for Combating Climate Change" was introduced, drawing inspiration from Islamic ethics, values, and legal principles. The "eco-friendly fatwa declares all activities that harm climate prohibited (Haram)" (AhramOnline, 2022).

Idllalène (2021, p. 37) presents an extensive list of globally issued *fatāwā*, which collectively contribute to the discourse surrounding environmental preservation and sustainability. This compilation offers a diverse array of perspectives and rulings that underscore the importance of safeguarding the natural world. In addressing environmental issues, the approach of issuing *fatwas* should not be interpreted as a means of forcing Muslims to comply with certain behaviors. Rather, seeking *fatwa*s or legal opinions from scholars can serve as a way to raise awareness and help people understand the gravity of the environmental challenges. The purpose is to provide ethical guidance and promote responsible actions within the context of Islamic teachings. Moreover, *fatāwā* were never devoid of legal underpinnings, as mentioned in Section 6.2.

6.3 Muslim Efforts in Environmentalism

Several Muslim organizations in the US and Britain are actively engaged in environmentalism. Green Muslims D.C. (GMDC), Muslim Green Team (MGT), Reading Islamic Trust for the Environment (RITE), Sheffield Islamic Network for the Environment (ShINE), Wisdom in Nature (WiN), and Muslim Action for Development and the Environment (MADE) are involved in diverse environmental activities: theoretical and practical approaches and practices. They are also active in online campaigns to raise ecological awareness (Hancock, 2018).

Environmental activism ranges from daily life concerns such as noise pollution, sewage, and garbage to global concerns such as climate change and natural resource conservation (Hopkins, 2001). Ummah for Earth, established by Lebanese climate organizer Nouhad Awwadin in 2000 in the MENA region, is an interesting global initiative that seeks to raise awareness about the challenges of global climate change through a Muslim lens. It presents itself as an alliance-led effort with a primary focus on empowering Muslim communities facing crises. The initiative brings together different organizations, such as Greenpeace, Islamic Relief, and Eco-Islam, among others, to collaborate toward this goal. Ummah for Earth launched an initiative, "Green Mosque Initiative," the goal of which is to install renewable energy sources in mosques across Muslim countries. This initiative recognizes mosques as crucial in addressing environmental damage, inspiring sustainable behaviors, and fostering holistic well-being within the Muslim community (Ummah for Earth, 2023).

Initiated in 2021 by Iyad Abumoghli, the founding director of the United Nations Environment Programme's Faith for Earth project, "Al-Mizan: A Covenant for the Earth" is a Muslim-led effort under the UNEP Faith for the Earth Initiative. This project unites global Muslim thought leaders to address environmental challenges (UNEP, 2021). Al-Mizan represents a contemporary Islamic perspective on the environment, aiming to enhance collective efforts at the local, regional, and international levels to address climate change and other ecological challenges. This initiative seeks to involve Islamic scholars and Muslim institutions worldwide in the formulation and acceptance of this Call, serving as a global endeavor to raise awareness and promote an Islamic understanding of environmental issues.

The Qur'anic Botanic Garden, an endeavor launched in 2008 by the Qatar Foundation, represents a unique paradigm shift in the realm of botanical gardens by exclusively cultivating plant species mentioned in the Qur'an and the *ḥadīth* of the Prophet Muhammad. Qur'anic Botanic Garden's mission encompasses fostering knowledge dissemination, promoting conservation principles, and building appreciation for cultural traditions (Ministry of Qatar Foundation, 2023).

Furthermore, within the works of Muslim environmental ethicists and intellectuals, one encounters a range of thematic elements and terminologies such as "Eco-Islam," "Green Islam," "Green energy," "Shallow Ecology," "Deep Ecology," "Ecofeminism," "Green Muslims," "Eco-Halal," "Green Dinner," "Green Mosque," "Green Ramadan," "Green Hajj," "Green Iftar," and others. These distinctive concepts serve to emphasize the significance of community involvement and active participation in matters pertaining to environmental conservation (Schwenke, 2012; Sponsel, 2020).

In his book *Green Deen*, Ibrahim Abdul-Matin (2010) suggests how to act in an Islamic way that is both socially and environmentally responsible. The book highlights the interconnectedness between waste management, energy consumption, water resources, and food production. Rooted in the belief that individuals will be held accountable to their Creator, the book calls for a critical examination of economic injustice and the fundamental causes of environmental problems. It advocates for a new vision that embraces collaboration across communities and traditions, promoting policy reforms, community organizing, interfaith activism, and innovation. *Green Deen* offers valuable examples of eco-friendly practices, with a primary focus on enhancing the sustainability of mosques through reduced energy and water consumption (Matin, 2010, p. 60). Taking inspiration from the holy mosques of Makkah and Madīnah, where ablution water (*waḍū'*) is recycled, this guide advocates for similar practices in mosques, including the establishment of dedicated water recycling stations (Matin, 2010, p. 122). These stations enable the reuse of *wuḍū'* water to nourish surrounding vegetation, effectively conserving precious resources. Furthermore, *Green Deen* highlights the pivotal role of Green Mosques in combatting environmental pollution. Encouraging the use of eco-friendly alternatives to disposable plastic and paper plates (Matin, 2010, p. 68), frequently brought by Muslims for meals at mosques, represents one facet of this comprehensive approach. Collectively, these initiatives aim to minimize resource wastage, promote sustainability, and address environmental concerns.

Similar environmental efforts – independent and government-sponsored – are seen emerging in several Muslim-majority countries, such as Egypt, Turkey, Iran, Pakistan, Nigeria, and Malaysia (Foltz, 2005a, p. xii). The field of environmental programs, however, has predominantly followed conventional or mainstream approach, encompassing initiatives such as environmental education, awareness campaigns, and the utilization of mass media platforms. As such, there has been a notable absence of a visible Islamic environmentalism, with only a few thin groups standing as exceptions (Rice, 2006; Ugur, 2019;

Koehrsen, 2021). Several factors contribute to this disparity. First, there exists a gap between the teachings of Islam and the practices of Muslims, leading to a lack of integration between religious principles and environmental concerns. Additionally, a discernible gap persists between religious scholars and environmental experts, hindering the establishment of institutions and groups focused on Islamic environmentalism.

Education is integral to the development of the Islamic personality and is instrumental in overcoming societal challenges and achieving sustainable progress. However, faith-based environmental education (EE) is often lacking in school curricula in Muslim countries. While concepts of ecology and environment are covered in secular curricula, there is a need to integrate environmental values and practices into Islamic religious education. By doing so, students can gain a comprehensive understanding of environmental care and its application in their daily lives. In South Africa, notable examples of environmental education within Islamic institutions (*madāris*/*makātib*) exist in the curriculum. Developed by two leading religious bodies such as Madrasatul Quds and Jamiatul Ulema Taalimi Board, these curricula incorporate teachings of Islam and emphasize the qualities necessary for responsible environmental action. The scholar Mohamed, in her examination of Islamic pedagogy in ecoethics, points out that while the existing curricula align with the environmental teachings (*ta'līm*) of Islam and the development of responsible environmental behavior (*tarbiyyah*), they may fall short in emphasizing the transformative aspect (*ta'dīb*) of self and society (2014, p. 345). Similarly, in Indonesia, environmental education based on Islamic ideals are being imparted in many schools.

6.4 Interfaith Perspective

Contemporary interfaith environmental activism is worth mentioning. Globally, about 84 percent of the world's population identifies with a religious group (Sherwood, 2018); consequently, interfaith environmental initiators have a vital role to play in the globalized world. Recent interfaith efforts, including conferences, workshops, and forums, are positive signs toward a collective faith-based activism.

The Muslim Declaration on Nature (Naseef, 1986) resulted from the first interreligious conference on nature preservation, which was held in Assisi, Italy, in 1986 and was sponsored by WWF International. Following the meeting, leaders from the world's five major religions (Buddhism, Christianity, Hinduism, Islam, and Judaism) released declarations addressing the subject of nature conservation from a religious perspective. In 2010, the Royal Aal al-Bayt Institute for Islamic Thought, based in Jordan, brought together Muslim and

Christian scholars to explore religious views on the environment with a focus on consumption and material development (Mattson, *et al.*, 2011).

Conclusions

Presently, Muslim societies confront similar environmental challenges as other developing nations. Multiple factors have been invoked to explain such a lack of concern for the environment. Some attribute the crisis to the historical context of European colonization and maritime trade, others point to the impact of overreliance on modern technology. Additionally, Muslim societies have been preoccupied with addressing pressing sociopolitical challenges, leaving limited space for contemplation and action on environmental issues. Matters such as governance, economic development, social justice, and geopolitical conflicts have understandably dominated the attention and resources of Muslim societies, diverting focus away from environmental concerns. This preoccupation with urgent matters has resulted in a diminished prioritization of environmental problems and hindered the implementation of effective environmental policies and practices within these societies (Nasr, 2005, p. 70; Foltz, 2013, p. 674). In sum, attributing environmental degradation to a single cause would be inappropriate.

What emerges from this discussion is that Islamic tradition is rich in environmental concerns and provides a valuable framework and understanding of the relationship between nature and humankind from a holistic perspective, away from an exploitative or materialistic outlook.

Islamic environmental ethics stresses the unity in creation, and reminds humans of their duty as stewards to exercise their power in maintaining equilibrium and fulfilling their responsibilities toward the Earth. It advocates for maintaining balance, harmony, and environmental preservation, and emphasizes the need for responsible environmental practices. Acknowledging that human dominance over nature is temporary and subject to ethical constraints, Islamic environmentalism has the potential to mitigate the current environmental crises, including climate change, and to provide a viable roadmap to move forward progressively without exploiting the environment. This could be achieved through Islamic environmental ethics in consonance with modern science and legal opinions.

The results of this study lead to the following urgent recommendations:

- In harmony with Islamic environmentalism, or "eco-theology," nature-friendly policies and activities should be adopted and encouraged.
- *'Ulama*, scholars, and opinion makers of the Muslim world must raise general awareness of the religious and ethical underpinnings of the environmental

protection goals based on the principles of *tawḥīd*, *khilāfah*, *amānah*, *ākhirah*, *fiṭrah*, and *mīzān*.

- Community involvement in environment-related programs is crucial for the emergence of an urgently needed "Green Movement" – "Green activism and Green lifestyle" – to develop a pro-environmental attitude and behavior among the public.
- A deeper exploration and analysis of the Muslim faith, particularly through Islamic sources, helps uncover many fruitful and constructive devices contributing to a possible redressing of humans' exploitative and materialistic tendencies.
- Scholars and activists should endeavor to identify and develop effective means of practical and functional cooperation to mitigate environmental pollution in all its forms, especially climate change and global warming.
- Academic institutions should be established to develop the study of Islamic environmentalism, such as the UK-based IFEES (Islamic Foundation for Ecology and Environmental Sciences) and the Qatar-based CILE (Centre for Islamic Legislation and Ethics).
- A three-tiered integrated religious–scientific–legal model is proposed, with Islamic ethical principles serving as the main fulcrum, interacting with the other two domains: science and law. Islamic ethics could help individuals to change their behavior and attitude concerning the environment. Through science, various environment-friendly activities such as recycling, biomass utilization, reforestation, and the use of modern technology for environmental goals may be achieved. Finally, specific legislation is indispensable to bolster and support the other two domains.
- Environmental education at all levels is essential to bring about positive behavioral changes to make daily life activities eco-friendly.
- Finally, interfaith initiatives on environmental preservation are highly recommended.

References

Abed, G. T & Davoodi, H. R. (2003). Challenges of Growth and Globalization in the Middle East and North Africa. International Monetary Fund. https://imf.org/external/pubs/ft/med/2003/eng/abed.htm.

Abrahamov, B. (2015). *Ibn al-'Arabī's Fuṣūṣ al-Ḥikam: An Annotated Translation of "The Bezels of Wisdom."* New York: Routledge.

Acea. (2022). World Motor Vehicle Production. www.acea.auto/figure/world-motor-vehicle-production/.

Agwan, A. R. (2000). Environment. In N. K. Singh & A. R. Agwan, eds., *Encyclopaedia of the Qur'ān*, Vol. 1. Delhi: Global Vision Publishing House.

Ahmad, A. (1997). *Islam and the Environmental Crisis*. London: Ta-ha.

Ahmad, A. (2009). Global Ethics, Environmentally Applied: An Islamic View. In King-tak Ip, ed., *Environmental Ethics: Intercultural*. Amsterdam: Rodopi, pp. 93–114.

Ahmad, I. (2001). *Musnad Ahmad*, ed., Shuaib al-Arnauti, 50 Vols. Beirut: Mu'asasah al-Risālah, Vol. 20.

AhramOnline. (2022). Dar El-Ifta International Conference Launches Fatwa Charter to Confront Climate Change. https://english.ahram.org.eg.

Al- 'Arabī, A. A. (1998). *Al-'Awāṣim min al-Qawāṣim fi Taḥqīq Mawāqif al-Ṣahābah Ba'da Wafāt al-Nabī*. Saudi Arabia: Ministry of Islamic Affairs, Dawah and Guidance.

Al-Attas, S. M. N. (1985). *Islam, Secularism and the Philosophy of the Future*. London: Mansell.

Al-Bar, I. A. (1992). *Al-Istī'āb fī Ma'rifat al-Aṣḥāb*, 3 Vols. Beirut: Dar al-Jīl, Vol. 2.

Al-Bukhārī, I. (1997). *Ṣaḥīḥ al-Bukhārī*, translated by Muhammad Muhsin Khan, 9 Vols. Riyadh: Darussalam.

Al-Hassani, S. T. S., Woodcock, E. & Saoud, R. eds. (2007). *1001 Inventions: Muslim Heritage in Our World*. Great Britain: Foundation for Science, Technology and Civilisation.

Al-Jurjānī, A. (1983). *Kitāb al-Ta'rifāt*. Beirut: Dār Al-Kutub Al-'Ilmiyyah, pp. 24, 51.

Al-Maqrīzī. (1971). "*Imtā' al-Asmā*" [The Enjoyment of Listening]. Beirut: Dār al-Kutub al-'Ilmiyyah.

Al-Maydani, A. R. (1998). *Kitāb al-Ḥadarāt al-Islāmiyyah Assasahā wa Wasā'iluhā wa Ṣuwaru min Tatbiqāt al-Muslimīn Lahā wa Lamhāt min Ta'thīrihā fi Sā'ir al-Umam*. Dimashq: Dār al-Qalam.

Al-Nasā'ī, I. (2007). *Sunan Al-Nasā'ī*, translated by Nasiruddin al-Khattab, 6 Vols. Riyadh: Darussalam.

Al Rawi, M. (2002). Contribution of Ibn Sina to the Development of Earth Sciences. https://muslimheritage.com/ibn-sina-development-earth-sciences/.

Al-Ṭabarī, J. (1967). *Tārīkh al-Tabarī*, Beirut: Dār al-Turāth.

Al-Tirmidhī, I. (2007). *Jāmi'Al-Tirmidhī*, translated by Abu Khaliyl, 6 Vols. Riyadh: Darussalam.

Al-Zuḥaylī, M. M. (2006). *Al-Qawā'id al-Fiqhiyyah wa Taṭbīqātuhā fī al-Madhāhib al-Arba'ah*. Damascus: Dār al-Fikr.

Amirpur, K. (2021). And We Shall Save the Earth: Muslim Environmental Stewards. In E. Ehlers & K. Amirpur, eds., *Middle East and North Africa: Climate, Culture, and Conflicts*. Leiden: Brill, pp. 39–58.

Ammar, N. & Gray, A. (2017). Islamic Environmental Teachings Compatible with Ecofeminism? In J. Hart, ed., *The Wiley Blackwell Companion to Religion and Ecology*. Oxford: Wiley Blackwell, pp. 301–314.

Ammar, N. (2001). Islam and Deep Ecology. In D. Barnhill & R. Gottlieb, eds., *Deep Ecology and World Religions*. Albany: State of New York Press, pp. 193–211.

Ammar, N. (2004). An Islamic Response to the Manifest Ecological Crisis: Issues of Justice. In R. S. Gottlieb, ed., *This Sacred Earth: Religion, Nature, Environment*, 2nd ed. New York: Routledge, pp. 256–268.

Ammar, N. (2005). Islam and Eco-Justice. In B. R. Taylor, ed., *The Encyclopedia of Religion and Nature*. London: Thoemmes Continuum, pp. 862–866.

Angluelov, N. (2016). *Fast Fashion and Its Negative Impact on Environment and Society*. London: Taylor & Francis.

Atil, E. (1981). *Kalila wa Dimna: Fables from a Fourteenth-Century Arabic Manuscript*. Washington, DC: Smithsonian Institution Press.

'Aṭṭār, F. (1971). *Conference of the Birds (Mantiq ut-tair): A Philosophical Religious Poem in Prose*. Colorado: Shambhala.

Attfield, R. (1999). *The Ethics of the Global Environment*. Edinburgh: Edinburgh University Press.

Attfield, R. (2001). Christainity. In D. Jameison, ed., *A Companion to Environmental Philosophy*. Massachusetts: Blackwell, pp. 96–110.

Attfield, R. (2003). Can Environmental Ethics Make a Difference? In R. Attfield, ed., *Environmental Ethics: An Overview for the Twenty-First Century*. Cambridge: Polity Press, pp. 75–84.

Attfield, R. (2016). *The Ethics of the Environment*. New York: Routledge.

Attfield, R. (2017). *Wonder, Value and God*. New York: Routledge.

Attfield, R. (2018). *Environmental Ethics: A Very Short Introduction*. Oxford: Oxford University Press.

Austin, J. E. & Bruch, C. E., eds. (2000). *The Environmental Consequences of War: Legal, Economic, and Scientific Perspectives*. Cambridge: Cambridge University Press.

Azad, A. K. (1971). *Tarjumān al-Qur'ān*. Delhi: Sahitya Academy.

Bagader, A. A., Al-Sabbagh, A. T. E., Al-Glenid, M. A., Izzidien, M. Y. S. & Llewellyn, O. A. (1994). Environmental Protection in Islam, *IUCN Environmental Policy and Law Paper*, 20, 2nd revised ed., Switzerland: IUCN.

Bagir, Z. A. & Martiam, N. (2017). Islam: Norms and Practices. In W. Jenkins, M. E. Tucker & J. Grim, eds., *Routledge Handbook of Religion and Ecology*. New York: Routledge, pp. 79–87.

Baker, I. (1998). The Flight of Time, Ecology and Islam. In H. A. Haleem, ed., *Islam and the Environment*. London: Ta-Ha, pp. 75–89.

Bassett, L., Brinkman, J. T. & Pedersen, K. P., eds. (2000). *Earth and Faith: A Book of Reflection for Action*. New York: Interfaith Partnership for the Environment/United Nations Environment Programme.

Bookchin, M. (1982). *The Ecology of Freedom: The Emergence and Dissolution of Hierarchy*. California: Cheshire Books.

Bratton, S. P. (2021). *Religion and the Environment: An Introduction*. New York: Routledge.

Brennan, A. & Yeuk-Sze, L. (2002). Environmental Ethics. In E. N. Zalta, ed., *The Stanford Encyclopedia of Philosophy*. Stanford University: Mmetaphysics Research Lab. http://plato.stanford.edu/archives/sum2002/entries/ethics-environmental.

Brimblecombe, P. & Nicholas, F. M. (1993). Case Study: The History and Ethics of Clean Air. In R. J. Berry, ed., *Environmental Dilemmas: Ethics and decisions*. London: Chapman & Hall, pp. 72–84.

Brown, D. A. (2001). The Ethical Dimensions of Global Environmental Issues. *Dædalus: Journal of The American Academy of Arts and Sciences*, 130(4), 59–76.

Brown, L. R. (2000). How Water Scarcity Will Shape the New Century – Earth Policy Institute [EPI]. www.earth-policy.org.

Burckhardt, T. (2009). *Art of Islam: Language and Meaning*. Foreword by Seyyed Hossein Nasr. Indiana: World Wisdom.

Callicott, J. B. (2017). Philosophy. In W. Jenkins, M. E., Tucker & J. Grim, eds., *Routledge Handbook of Religion and Ecology*. New York: Routledge, pp. 364–374.

Campanini, M. (2015). Science and Epistemology in Medieval Islam. *Social Epistemology Review and Reply Collective*, 4(12), 20–28.

Carson, R. (1963). *Silent Spring*. London: Hamish Hamilton.

Centre for Climate and Energy Solutions (C2ES). (2023). Global Emissions. https:c2es.org/content/international-emissions/.

Chant, C. and Goodman, D., eds. (1999). *Pre-Industrial Cities and Technology*. London: Routledge.

Chasek, P. S. & Downie, D. L. (2018). *Global Environmental Politics*. New York: Routledge.

Chishti, S. K. K. (2003). Fitra: An Islamic Model for Humans and the Environment. In R. C. Foltz, F. M. Denny & A. Baharuddin, eds., *Islam and Ecology: A Bestowed Trust*. Cambridge: Harvard University Press, pp. 67–82.

Chittick, W. (1986). God Surrounds All Things: An Islamic Perspective on the Environment. *The World & I*, 1(6), 671–678.

Clarke, L. (2003). The Universe Alive: Nature in the *Masnavi* of Jalal al-Din Rumi. In R. C. Foltz, F. M. Denny & A. Baharuddin, eds., *Islam and Ecology: A Bestowed Trust*. Cambridge: Harvard University Press, pp. 39–66.

Cleveland Museum of Natural History. (2020). How Do Natural Disasters Affect Biodiversity? https://cmnh.org/science-news/blog/january-2020/how-do-natural-disasters-affect-biodiversity.

Conca, K. & Dabelko, G. D. (2019). *Green Planet Blues: Critical Perspectives on Global Environmental Politics*. New York: Routledge.

D'Eaubonne, F. (2022). *Feminism or Death: How the Women's Movement Can Save the Planet*, trans. Ruth Hottell. New York: Verso.

Dalton, A. M. & Simmons, H. C. (2010). *Ecotheology and the Practice of Hope*. Albany: State University of New York Press.

Dāwūd, A. (2008). *Sunan Abū Dāwūd*, translated by Yaser Qadi, 5 Vols. Riyadh: Darussalam.

Deen. M. Y. I. (2004). Islamic Environmental Ethics, Law, and Society. In R. S. Gottlieb, ed., *This Sacred Earth: Religion, Nature, Environment*, 2nd ed. New York: Routledge, pp. 142–149.

DeGregori, T. R. (2002). *The Environment, Our Natural Resources, and Modern Technology*. Ames: Lowa State University Press.

DeLong-Bas, N. (2018). Islam, Nature, and the Environment. *Oxford Bibliographies*. www.oxfordbibliographies.com/view/document.

Desjardins, J. R. (2013). *Environmental Ethics: An Introduction to Environmental Philosophy*. Boston: Wadsworth.

Díaz, M. D. (2021). Ṣūfism. In M. A. Upal & C. M. Cusack, eds., *Handbook of Islamic Sects and Movements*. Leiden: Brill, pp. 517–542.

Dickson, B. (2000). The Ethicist Conception of Environmental Problems. *Environmental Values*, 9, 127–152.

Dien, M. Y. I. (2000). *The Environmental Dimensions of Islam*. Cambridge: Lutterworth Press.

Droz, L. (2022). *The Concept of Milieu in Environmental Ethics: Individual Responsibility within an Interconnected World*. New York: Routledge.

Dutton, Y. (1998). Islam and the Environment: A Framework for Enquiry. In H. A. Haleem, ed., *Islam and the Environment*. London: Ta-Ha, pp. 56–74.

Edis, T. (2008). Modern Science and Conservative Islam: An Uneasy Relationship. *Science and Education*, 18 (6–7), 985–903.

Ehrlich, P. (1968). *The Population Bomb*. New York: Ballantine Books.

El-Bizri, N. ed. (2008). *Epistles of the Brethren of Purity: The Ikhwan al-Safa' and their Rasa'il*. Oxford: Oxford University Press.

Elwazani, S. A. (1995). Sacral Qualities of Form in Mosque Architecture. *American Journal of Islam and Society*, 12(4), 478–495.

Everard, M. (2013). *The Hydropolitics of Dams: Engineering or Ecosystems?* London: Zed Books.

Foltz, R. C. (2003). Islamic Environmentalism: A Matter of Interpretation. In R. C. Foltz, F. M. Denny & A. Baharuddin, eds., *Islam and Ecology: A Bestowed Trust*. Cambridge: Harvard University Press, pp. 249–275.

Foltz, R., ed. (2005a). *Environmentalism in the Muslim World*. New York: Nova Science, pp. vii–xiii.

Foltz, R. (2005b). Islam. In B. R. Taylor, ed., *The Encyclopedia of Religion and Nature*. London: Thoemmes Continuum, pp.858–862.

Foltz, R. (2006c). "This She-Camel of God is a Sign to You": Dimensions of Animals in Islamic Tradition and Muslim Culture. In P. Waldau & K. Patton, eds., *A Communion of Subjects: Animals in Religion, Science, and Ethics*. New York: Columbia University Press, pp. 149–160.

Foltz, R. (2013). Ecology in Islam. In A. L. C. Runehov & L. Oviedo, eds., *Encyclopedia of Sciences and Religions*. Dordrecht: Springer, pp. 670–678.

Foltz, R. C. (2006a). Islam. In R. S. Gottlieb, ed., *The Oxford Handbook of Religion and Ecology*. New York: Oxford University Press, pp. 207–219.

Foltz, R. C. (2006b). *Animals in Islamic Tradition and Muslim Cultures*. Oxford: Oneworld.

Gade, A. M. (2019). *Muslim Environmentalism: Religious and Social Foundations*. New York: Columbia University Press.

Gari, L. (2002). Arabic Treatises on Environmental Pollution up to the End of the Thirteenth Century. *Environment and History*, 8 (4), 475–488.

Gari, L. (2006). A History of the Hima Conservation System. *Environment and History*, 12(2), 213–228. https://muslimheritage.com/ecology-muslim-heritage-history-hima-conservsyst/#ftnref23.

Gershon, L. (2019). Rachel Carson's Critics Called Her a Witch. *JSTOR Daily*. https://daily.jstor.org/rachel-carsons-critics-called-her-a-witch/.

Gillette, P. R. (2005). How Science Can Help Religion Benefit Society. *Zygon: Journal of Religion and Science*, 40(2), 299–305.

Glasbergen, P. & Blower, A. (1995). *Environmental Policy in an International Context: Perspectives on Environmental Problems*. Oxford: Butterworth-Heinemann.

Goodman, L. E. (1972). *Ibn Tufayl's Hayy ibn Yaqzān: A Philosophical Tale*, translated with introduction and notes by L. E. Goodman. New York: Twayne.

Graham, W. A. (2014). The Qur'ān as a Discourse of Signs. In A. Korangy & D. J. Scheffield, eds., *No Tapping around Philology: A Festschrift in Honor of Wheeler McIntosh Thackston Jr.'s 70th Birthday*. Wiesbaden: Harrassowitz Verlag, pp. 263–275.

Graham, W. A. (2016). *Islamic and Comparative Religious Studies: Selected Writings*. New York: Routledge.

Guessoum, N. (2011). *Islam's Quantum Question: Reconciling Muslim Tradition and Modern Science*. London: I. B. Tauris.

Guha-Sapir, D, Hargitt, D. & Hoyois P. (2004). Thirty Years of Natural Disasters 1974–2003: The Numbers. Belgium: Centre for Research on the Epidemiology of Disasters (CRED).

Haddad, M. (2021a). Water Supply, Sanitation, Hygienic Considerations and Practices in Muslim Civilizations. https://muslimheritage.com/water-supply-sanitation/.

Haddad, M. (2021b). Pro-Environmental Practices in Muslim Civilization. https://muslimheritage.com/pro-environmental/.

Haider, S. G. (1984). Habitat and Values in Islam: A Conceptual Formulation of an Islamic City. In Z. Sardar, ed., *The Touch of Midas: Science, Values and the Environment in Islam and the West*. Manchester: University of Manchester Press, pp. 170–208.

Hamed, S. A. (1993). Seeing the Environment through Islamic Eyes: Application of Shariah to Natural Resources Planning and Management. *Journal of Agricultural and Environmental Ethics*, 6(2), 145–164.

Hamed, S. A. (2003). Capacity Building for Sustainable Development: The Dilemma of Islamization of Environmental Institutions. In R. C. Foltz, F. M. Denny & A. Baharuddin, eds., *Islam and Ecology: A Bestowed Trust*. Cambridge: Harvard University Press, pp. 403–421.

Hancock, R. (2018). *Islamic Environmentalism: Activism in the United States and Great Britain*. London: Routledge.

Haq, S. N. (2001a). Islam. In D. Jamieson, ed., *A Companion to Environmental Philosophy*. Oxford: Blackwell, pp. 111–129.

Haq, S. N. (2001b). Islam and Ecology: Toward Retrieval and Reconstruction. *Daedalus: Journal of the American Academy of Arts and Sciences*, 130(4), 141–177.

Haq, S. N. (2003). Islam and Ecology: Towards Retrieval and Reconstruction. In R. C. Foltz, F. M. Denny & A. Baharuddin, eds., *Islam and Ecology: A Bestowed Trust*. Cambridge: Harvard University Press, pp. 121–154.

Hardin, G. (1968). The Tragedy of the Commons. *Science*, 162(3859), 1243–1248.

Ḥazm, I. (1994). *The Ring of the Dove: A Treatise on the Art and Practice of Arab Love*. Tr. A. J. Arberry. London: Luzac Oriental.

Hemmati, M. (2003). Gender-Specific Patterns of Poverty and (Over-) Consumption in Developing and Developed Countries. In E. Jochem, J. Sathaye & D. Bouille, eds., *Society, Behaviour, and Climate Change Mitigation*, Vol. 8. New York: Kluwer Academic, pp. 169–190.

Hens, L. & Susanne, C. (1998). Environmental Ethics. *Global Bioethics*, 2(1–4), 97–118.

Hiller, A. (2017). Consequentialism in Environmental Ethics. In S. M. Gardiner & A. Thompson, eds., *The Oxford Handbook of Environmental Ethics*. New York: Oxford University Press, pp. 199–210.

Hobson, I. (1998). Guiding Principles for a Solution to Environmental Problems. In H. A. Haleem, ed., *Islam and the Environment*. London: Ta-Ha, pp. 33–42.

Hopkins, N. S., Mehanna, S. R. & El-Haggar, S. (2001). *People and Pollution: Cultural Construction and Social Action in Egypt*. Cairo: American University in Cairo Press.

Idllalène, S. (2021). *Rediscovery and Revival in Islamic Environmental Law*. Cambridge: Cambridge University Press.

International Islamic Climate Change Symposium (IICCS). (2015). *Islamic Declaration on Global Climate Change*. http://islamicclimatedeclaration .org/islamic-declaration-on-global-clim.

Irawan, B., Nasution, I. F. A. & Coleman, H. (2021). Applying Ibn 'Arabī's Concept of *Tajallī*: A Sufi Approach to Environmental Ethics. *Teosofia: Indonesian Journal of Islamic Mysticism*, 10(1), 21–36.

Islam, M. S. (2012). Old Philosophy, New Movement: The Rise of the Islamic Ecological Paradigm in the Discourse of Environmentalism. *Nature and Culture*, 7 (1), 72–94.

Jamieson, D. (2008). *Ethics and the Environment: An Introduction*. Cambridge: Cambridge University Press, pp. 93–111.

Jamil, S. (2022). Halal Wastewater Recycling: Environmental Solution or Religious Complication? In J. Köhrsen, J. Blanc & F. Huber, eds., *Religious Environmental Activism Emerging Conflicts and Tensions in Earth Stewardship*. London: Routledge, pp. 93–11.

Jenkins, W. (2005). Islamic Law and Environmental Ethics: How Jurisprudence ("Usul Al-Fiqh") Mobilizes Practical Reform. *Worldviews*, 9(3), 338–364.

Johnson-Davies, D. (tr.). (1994). *The Island of Animals*. London: Quartet Books.

Johnston, D. L. (2012). Intra-Muslim Debates on Ecology: Is Shari'a Still Relevant? *Worldviews*, 16(3), 218–238.

Just, R. E. & Netanyahu, S., eds. (1998). *Conflict and Cooperation on Trans-Boundary Water Resources*. New York: Springer Science.

Kaltner, J. (2011). *Introducing the Qur'an for Today's Reader*. Minneapolis: Fortress Press.

Kamali, M. H. (2012). Environmental Care in Islamic Teaching. *Islam and Civilizational Renewal*, 3(2), 261–283.

Kamali, M. H. (2016). Islam and the Environment: An Examination of the Source Evidence. In M. H. Kamali, O. Bakar, D. A. Batchelor & R. Hashim, eds., *Islamic Perspectives on Science and Technology* (Selected Conference Papers). Singapore: Springer, pp. 171–192.

Kameri-Mbote, P. (2007). Water, Conflict, and Cooperation: Lessons from the Nile River Basin. *Navigating Peace* (isuue no. 04 (January)). Washington: Woodrow Wilson International Center for Scholars.

Kanagaraj, P. & Thanikodi, A. (2009). Military Technologies and Environmental Rights: A Study of Deleterious Consequences and Remedial Measures. *The Indian Journal of Political Science*, 70(2), 351–362.

Kathīr, I. (1999). *Tafsīr Qur'ān al-'Aẓīm*. Riyāḍ: Dār Tayyibah li al-Nashr wa al-Tawzī'.

Kawall, J. (2017). A History of Environmental Ethics. In S. M. Gardiner & A. Thompson, eds., *The Oxford Handbook of Environmental Ethics*. New York: Oxford University Press, pp. 13–26.

Kevin C. E. (2017). The Ethics of Environmental Pollution. In S. M. Gardiner & A. Thompson, eds., *The Oxford Handbook of Environmental Ethics*. New York: Oxford University Press, pp. 369–379.

Khadduri, M. (2012). Maṣlaḥa. In P. Bearman, T. Bianquis, C. E. Bosworth, E. V. Donzel & W. P. Heinrichs, eds., *Encyclopaedia of Islam*, 2nd ed. Leiden: E. J. Brill, p. 738. http://dx.doi.org/10.1163/1573-3912_islam_SIM_5019.

Khaldun, I. (2005). *The Muqaddimah*, trans. Franz Rosenthal. New Jersey: Princeton University Press.

Khalid, F. (1992). The Disconnected People. In F. Khalid and O'Brien, eds., *Islam and Ecology*. London: Cassell, pp. 99–111.

Khalid, F. (1998). Islam, Ecology and the World Order. In H. A. Haleem, ed., *Islam and the Environment*. London: Ta-Ha, pp. 16–31.

Khalid, F. (2002). Islam and the Environment. In P. Timmerman, ed., *Social and Economic Dimensions of Global Environmental Change*. Chichester: Wiley, Vol. 5, pp. 332–339.

Khalid, F. (2003). Islam, Ecology and Modernity: An Islamic Critique of the Root Causes of Environmental Degradation. In R. C. Foltz, F. M. Denny & A. Baharuddin, eds., *Islam and Ecology: A Bestowed Trust*. Cambridge: Harvard University Press, pp. 229–321.

Khalid, F. (2005). Islamic Basis for Environmental Protection. In B. R. Taylor, ed., *The Encyclopedia of Religion and Nature*. London: Thoemmes Continuum, pp. 879–883.

Khalid, F. (2017). Exploring Environmental Ethics in Islam: Insights from the Qur'an and the Practice of Prophet Muhammad. In J. Hart, ed., *The Wiley Blackwell Companion to Religion and Ecology*. Oxford: Wiley Blackwell, pp. 130–145.

Khalid, F. (2019). *Signs on the Earth: Islam, Modernity and the Climate Crisis*. Markfield: Kube.

Koehrsen, J. (2021). Muslims and Climate Change: How Islam, Muslim Organizations, and Religious Leaders Influence Climate Change Perceptions and Mitigation Activities. *WIREs Climate Change*, 12(3), 1–19.

Kreame, D. K. (2012). The Past, Present, and Future of Water Conflict and International Security. *Journal of Contemporary Water Research & Education*, 149, 88–96.

Kula, E. (2001). Islam and Environmental Conservation. *Environmental Conservation*, 28(1), 1–9.

Lai, O. (2021). 10 Deforestation Facts You Should Know about. Earth.org. https://earth.org/deforestation-facts/.

Leopold, A. (1949). *A Sand County Almanac, and Sketches Here and There*. New York: Oxford University Press.

Lings, M. (1975). *What Is Sufism?* California: University of California Press.

Llewellyn, O. A. (2003). The Basis for a Discipline of Islamic Environmental Law. In R. C. Foltz, F. M. Denny & A. Baharuddin, eds., *Islam and Ecology: A Bestowed Trust*. Cambridge: Harvard University Press, pp. 185–247.

Llewellyn, U. R. (1985). Islamic Jurisprudence and Environmental Planning. *Journal of Research in Islamic Economics*, 2(1), 27–46.

London, J. & White, G. F. (2019). The Environmental Effects of Nuclear War: An Overview. In J. London & G. F. White, eds., *The Environmental Effects of Nuclear War*. New York: Routledge, pp. 1–17.

Lubis, A. (1998). Environmental Ethics in Islam. *Cross Boundaries*. http://mandailing.org/Eng/envethics.html.

Lundberg, E. (2019). Facing Our Global Environmental Challenges Requires Efficient International Cooperation. *UN Environmental Programme*. www.unep.org/news-and-stories/editorial/facing-our-global-environmental-challenges-requires-efficient.

Mājah, I. (2007). *Sunan Ibn Mājah*, translated by Abu Khaliyl, 5 Vols. Riyadh: Darussalam.

Mālik, I. (2014). *Muwaṭṭa'*, translated by Aisha Bewley. Norwich: Diwan Press.

Manzoor, S. P. (1984). Environment and Values: The Islamic Perspective. In Z. Sardar, ed., *The Touch of Midas: Science, Values and the Environment in Islam and the West*. Manchester: University of Manchester Press, pp. 150–169.

Mary, E. T. (2006). Religion and Ecology: Survey of the Field. In R. S. Gottlieb, ed., *The Oxford Handbook of Religion and Ecology*. New York: Oxford University Press, pp. 399–418.

Masri, A. B. A. (2007). *Animal Welfare in Islam*. Markfield: Islamic Foundation.

Matin, I. A. (2010). *Green Deen: What Islam Teaches about Protecting the Planet*. San Francisco: Berrett-Koehler.

Mattson, I., Hofmann, M. W., Arneth, M. & Mieth, D. (2011). *Islam, Christianity & the Environment*. Jordan: The Royal Aal Al-Bayt Institute for Islamic Thought.

Maududi, A. A. (2013). *Towards Understanding the Qur'an [English Version of Tafhīm al-Qur'ān]*. Trans. and ed., Zafar Isḥāq Anṣārī. MMI: New Delhi.

McKibben, B. (1999). Indifferent to a Planet in Pain. *The New York Times*. www.nytimes.com/1999/09/04/opinion/indifferent-to-a-planet-in-pain.html.

Michell, G, ed. (2011). *Architecture of the Islamic World: Its History and Social Meaning*. London: Thames & Hudson.

Mies, M. (2017). Deceiving the Third World: The Myth of Catching-Up Development. In L. P. Pojman, P. Pojman & K. McShane, eds., *Environmental Ethics: Readings in Theory and Application*, 7th ed. Boston: Cengage Learning, pp. 341–349.

Ministry of Awqaf. (2005). *Al-Mawsū'ah al-Fiqhiyyah* [Encyclopedia of Islamic Jurisprudence], Vol. 32. Kuwait: Ministry of Awqaf.

Ministry of Qatar Foundation. (2023). Quranic Botanic Garden. https://qbg.org.qa/.

Mohamed, N. (2014). Capturing Green Curriculum Spaces in the Maktab: Implications for Environmental Teaching and Learning. In J. D. Chapma, S. McNamara, M. J. Reiss & Y. Waghid, eds., *International Handbook of Learning, Teaching and Leading in Faith-Based Schools*. New York: Springer, pp. 335–351.

Mohamed, N. (2017). Revitalizing Islamic Ecological Ethics through Education. In M. A. Peters, eds., *Encyclopedia of Educational Philosophy and Theory*. Singapore: Springer, pp. 2038–2043.

Mohamed, Y. (1995).The Interpretations of Fiṭrah. *Islamic Studies*, 34(2), 129–151.

Moosa, E. (2020). Qur'anic Ethics. In M. Shah & M. A. Haleem, eds., *The Oxford Handbook of Qur'anic Studies*. Oxford: Oxford University Press, pp. 464–472.

Mortada, H. (2003). *Traditional Islamic Principles of Built Environment*. London: RoutledgeCurzon.

Muslim, I. (2007). *Ṣaḥīḥ Muslim*, translated by Nasiruddin al-Khattab, 7 Vols. Riyadh: Darussalam, p. 112.

Naess, A. (1973). The Shallow and the Deep, Long-Range Ecology Movement. *Inquiry*, 16(1–4), 95–100.

Naess, A. (1987). Self-Realization: An Ecological Approach to Being in the World. *The Trumpeter*, 4(3), 35–41.

Naseef, A. O. (1986). *The Muslim Declaration on Nature. A: The Assisi Declarations: Messages on Humanity and Nature from Buddhism, Christianity, Hinduism, Islam & Judaism*. Basilica di S. Francesco Assisi, Italy, pp. 10–13.

Naseef, A. O. (1998). The Muslim Declaration on Nature. In H. A. Haleem, ed., *Islam and the Environment*. London: Ta-Ha, pp. 12–15.

Nash, R. F. (1989). *The Rights of Nature: A History of Environmental Ethics*. Madison: The University of Wisconsin Press.

Nasr, S. H. (1964 [1978]). *An Introduction to Islamic Cosmological Doctrines: Conceptions of Nature and Methods Used for Its Study by the Ikhwān al-Ṣafā', al-Birūnī, and Ibn Sīnā*, rev. ed. London: Thames & Hudson.

Nasr, S. H. (1975[2001]). *Islam and the Plight of Modern Man*, rev. ed. Chicago: ABC International Group.

Nasr, S. H. (1990). Islam and Environmental Crisis. *MAAS Journal Islamic Science*, 6(2), 31–51.

Nasr, S. H. (1992). Islam and the Environmental Crisis. In S. C. Rockefeller, ed., *Spirit and Nature: Why the Environment Is a Religious Issue*. Boston: Beacon Press, pp. 84–108.

Nasr, S. H. (1996). *Religion and the Order of Nature*. New York: Oxford University Press.

Nasr, S. H. (1998). Sacred Science and the Environmental Crisis: An Islamic Perspective. In H. A. Haleem, ed., *Islam and the Environment*. London: Ta-Ha, pp. 118–148.

Nasr, S. H. (2003). Islam, the Contemporary Islamic World and the Environmental Crisis. In R. C. Foltz, , F. M. Denny & A. Baharuddin, eds., *Islam and Ecology*. Cambridge: Harvard University Press, pp. 85–106.

Nasr, S. H. (2005). *The Need for a Sacred Science*. Richmond: Curzon Press.

Nasr, S. H. (2020). The Environmental Crisis in the Islamic World – Pertinence of the Teachings of Traditional Islam. In M. Abbas, Z. Iqbal & S. K. Sadr, eds., *Handbook of Ethics of Islamic Economics and Finance*. Berlin: De Gruyter, pp. 156–165.

Nasr, S. H. (1990 [1968]). *Man and Nature: The Spiritual Crisis of Modern Man*. London: Unwin Paperbacks.

Nawaz, R. (2019). Water innovations in the Muslim world: past glories and future outlook. Manchester: The Foundation for Science, Technology and Civilisation. https://muslimheritage.com/water-innovations-in-the-muslim-world-past-glories-and-future-outlook/.

Nelson, S. A. (2018). Natural Hazards and Natural Disasters. www2.tulane.edu/~sanelson/Natural_Disasters/introduction.htm.

Nizamoglu, C. (2007). Cats in Islamic Culture. https://muslimheritage.com/cats-islamic-culture/#ftnref108.

Norton, B. G. (1984). Environmental Ethics and Weak Anthropocentrism. *Environmental Ethics*, 6(2), 131–148.

Obiedat, A. Z. (2022). *Modernity and the Ideals of Arab-Islamic and Western-Scientific Philosophy: The Worldviews of Mario Bunge and Taha Abd al-Rahman*. New York: Palgrave Macmillan.

Olivier, J. G. J. & Peters, J. A. H. W. (2020). Trends in Global CO2 and Total Greenhouse Gas Emissions: 2020 Report. The Hague: PBL Netherlands Environmental Assessment Agency.

Ouis, S. P. (1998). Islamic Ecotheology Based on the Qur'ān. *Islamic Studies*, 37(2), 151–181.

Ouis, S. P. (2003). Global Environmental Relations: An Islamic Perspective. *The Muslim Lawyer*, 4(1), 1–7. www.aml.org.uk/journal/4.1/SPO%20%20Global%20Environment%20Relations.pdf.

Özdemir, I. (2003). Toward an Understanding of Environmental Ethics from a Qur'anic Perspective. In R. C. Foltz, F. M. Denny & A. Baharuddin, eds., *Islam and Ecology: A Bestowed Trust*. Cambridge: Harvard University Press, pp. 3–37.

Özdemir, I. (2008). *The Ethical Dimension of Human Attitude towards Nature – A Muslim Perspective*. Ankara: Insan.

Palmer, C. (2012). An Overview of Environmental Ethics. In L. P. Pojman & P. Pojman, eds., *Environmental Ethics: Readings in Theory and Application*. Boston: Clark Baxter, pp. 10–35.

Parvaiz, M. A. (2005). Islam on Man and Nature. In B. R. Taylor, ed., *The Encyclopedia of Religion and Nature*. London: Thoemmes Continuum, pp. 875–879.

Pew Research Centre [PEW]. (2011). The Future Global Muslim Population: Projections for 2010–2030. www.pewporm.org.

Pew Research Centre [PEW]. (2019). The Countries with the 10 Largest Christian Populations and the 10 Largest Muslim Populations. www.pew porm.org.

Quadir, T. M. (2013). *Traditional Islamic Environmentalism: The Vision of Seyyed Hossein Nasr*. Lanham: University Press of America.

Qudāmah, I. (1997). *Al-Mughnī*, Vol. 8. Riyāḍ: Dār al-'Ālim al-Kutub.

Ramadan, T. (2004). *Western Muslims and the Future of Islam*. New York: Oxford University Press.

Ramadan, T. (2009). *Radical Reform: Islamic Ethics and Liberation*. Oxford: Oxford University Press.

Ramadan, T. (2018). Islamic Ethics: Sources, Methodology and Application. In A. Bagheri & K. Alali, eds., *Islamic Bioethics: Current Issues & Challenges*. London: World Scientific Publishing Europe, pp. 1–22.

Ravnborg, H. M. (2003). From Water "Wars" to Water "Riots"?-Lessons from Transboundary Water Management. In J. Boesen & H. M. Ravnborg, eds., *Proceedings of the International Conference, December*. Copenhagen: DIIS, pp. 5–17.

Regan, T. (1979). An Examination and Defense of One Argument Concerning Animal Rights. *Inquiry*, 22, 189–219.

Regan, T. (1980). Animal Rights, Human Wrongs. *Environmental Ethics*, 2(2), 99–120.

Rice, G. (2006). Pro-environmental Behavior in Egypt: Is There a Role for Islamic Environmental Ethics? *Journal of Business Ethics*, 65, 373–390.

Robinson, C. A. (2002A). Development of an International Framework for the Protection of the Environment from the Effects of Ionizing Radiation. In *Protection of the Environment from Ionising Radiation: The Development and Application of a System of Radiation Protection for the Environment*. Austria: International Atomic Energy Agency, pp. 110–117.

Rodrigue, J. (2020). *The Geography of Transport Systems*, 5th ed. New York: Routledge.

Sachs, J. D., M. S. Sorondo, O. Flanagan, W. Vendley, A. Annett & J. Thorson (2022). *Ethics in Action for Sustainable Development*. New York: Columbia University Press.

Salam. I. A. (2015). *Qawā'id al-Aḥkām fī Maṣāliḥ al-An'ām*. Bayrūt: Dār al-Kutub al-'Ilmīyah.

Sandler, R. L. (2018). *Environmental Ethics: Theory in Practice*. New York: Oxford University Press.

Saniotis, A. (2012). Muslim and Ecology: Fostering Islamic Environmental Ethics. *Contemporary Islam*, 6(2), 155–171.

Sardar, Z. (1985). *Islamic Futures: The Shape of Ideas to Come*. New York: Mensell.

Sardar, Z. (2006). *How Do You Know? Reading Ziauddin Sardar on Islam, Science and Cultural Relations*, ed., E. Masood. London: Pluto Press.

Sayem, M. A. (2019). The Eco-philosophy of Seyyed Hossein Nasr: Spiritual Crisis and Environmental Degradation. *Islamic Studies*, 58(2), 271–295.

Schwenke, A. M. (2012). *Globalized Eco-Islam – A Survey of Global Islamic Environmentalism*. Leiden: Leiden Institute for Religious Studies.

Serageldin, I. (2010). Water Wars? A Talk with Ismail Serageldin. *World Policy Journal*, 26(4), 25–31.

Setia, A. (2007). The Inner Dimensions of Going Green: Articulating an Islamic Deep-Ecology. *Islam & Science*, 5(2), 117–150.

Sharp, A. M. (2015). Orthodox Christians, Muslims, and the Environment: The Case for a New Sacred Science, In D. Pratt, J. Hoover, J. Davies & J. A. Chesworth, eds., *The Character of Christian-Muslim Encounter: Essays in Honour of David Thomas*. Leiden: Brill, pp. 471–491.

Shervood, H. (2018). Religion: Why Faith Is Becoming More and More Popular. *The Guardian*. https://theguardian.com/news/2018/aug/27/religion-why-is-faith-growing-and-what-happens-next.

Shomali, M. (2008). Aspects of Environmental Ethics: An Islamic Perspective. www.thinkingfaith.org.

Singer, P. (1975). *Animal Liberation: A New Ethics for Our Treatment of Animals*. New York: Random House.

Singer, P. (1999). Ethics across the Species Boundary. In N. Low, ed., *Global Ethics and Environment*. New York: Routledge, pp. 146–157.

Smith, G., ed. (2017). *The War and Environment Reader*. Virginia: Just World Books.

Spencer, A. J. (2019). The Modernistic Roots of Our Ecological Crisis: The Lynn White Thesis at Fifty. *Journal of Markets & Morality*, 22(2), 355–371.

Sponsel, L. E. (2020). Introduction to "Religious Environmentalism Activism in Asia: Case Studies in Spiritual Ecology." *Religion*, 11(2), 1–6.

Stander, L. & Theodore, L. (2011). Environmental Implications of Nanotechnology – An Update. *International Journal of Environmental Research and Public Health*, 8(2), 470–479.

Stenmark, M. (2009). The Relevance of Environmental Ethical Theories for Policy Making. In B. A. Minteer, ed., *Nature in Common? Environmental Ethics and the Contested Foundations of Environmental Policy*. Philadelphia: Temple University Press, pp. 83–96.

Sylvan (Routley), R. (1973). Is There a Need for a New, an Environmental, Ethic? In R. Attfield, ed. [2008], *The Ethics of the Environment*. New York: Routledge, pp. 3–13.

Taylor, P. (1986). *Respect for Nature: A Theory of Environmental Ethics*. Princeton: Princeton University Press.

Taymiyyah, I. (1965). *Majmūʿ al-Fatāwā*. Bayrūt: Dār al-Maʿrifah.

The World Bank (WB). (2019). How Much Do Our Wardrobes Cost to the Environment? https://worldbank.org/en/news/feature/2019/09/23/costo-moda-medio-ambiente.

The World Counts. (2022). State of the Planet. www.theworldcounts.com/challenges/planet-earth/state-of-the-planet.

Thompson, A. (2017). Anthropocentrism: Humanity as Peril and Promise. In S. M. Gardiner & A. Thompson, eds., *The Oxford Handbook of Environmental Ethics*. New York: Oxford University Press, pp. 77–89.

Tiles, J. E. (2000). *Moral Measures: An Introduction to Ethics West and East*. London: Routledge.

Total Energy Consumption [TEC]. (2022). World Energy & Climate Statistics – Yearbook 2022, Enerdata. https://yearbook.enerdata.net/total-energy/world-consumption-statistics.html.

Toynbee, A. (1972). The Religious Background of the Present Environmental Crisis, *International Journal of Environmental Studies*, 3(1–4), 141–146.

Tucker, M. E. & Grim, J. (2017). The Movement of Religion and Ecology: Emerging Field and Dynamic Force. In W. Jenkins, M. E. Tucker & J. Grim, eds., *Routledge Handbook of Religion and Ecology*. New York: Routledge, pp. 3–11.

Tucker, M. E. & Grim, J. (2022). The Challenge of the Environmental Crisis: Yale Forum on Religion and Ecology. http://fore.research.yale.edu/publications/books/cswr/the-challengeof-the-environmental-crisis.

Tucker, M. E. & Grim, J. A. (2001). Introduction: The Emerging Alliance of World Religions and Ecology, Religion and Ecology: Can the Climate Change? *Dædalus*, 130(4), 1–22.

Ugur, Z. B. (2019). Are Muslims in Turkey Really "Green"? *Worldviews: Global Religions, Culture, and Ecology*, 23(3), 275–294.

Ummah for Earth. (2023). https://ummah4earth.org/en/about-ummah-for-earth/.

UNEP. (2021). Al-Mizan: A Covenant for the Earth. www.unep.org/al-mizan-covenant-earth.

UNEP. (n.d.). Religions and Environmental Protection. www.unep.org/about-un-environment-programme/faith-earth-initiative/religions-and-environmental-protection.

UNESCO. (1977). A Golden Age of Arab Culture. *The Unesco Courier*, 1–56.

UNESCO. (2012). Healthy Ocean, Healthy People, United Nations Conference on Sustainable Development. France: UNESCO.

Union of Concerned Scientists [UCS]. (2022). Each Country's Share of CO2 Emissions. www.ucsusa.org/resources/each-countrys-share-co2-emissions.

Vaughan-Lee, ed. (2013). *Spiritual Ecology: The Cry of the Earth*. California: The Golden Sufi Center.

Warren, K. J. (2000). *Ecofeminist Philosophy: A Western Perspective on What It Is and Why It Matters*. New York: Rowman & Littlefield.

Watling, T. (2009). *Ecological Imaginations in the World Religions: An Ethnographic Analysis*. London: Continuum International.

Watt, J. C., Wroniewicz, V. S., & Ioli, D. F. (1988). Environmental Concerns Associated with the Design of Genetic Engineering Facilities. In G. S. Omenn, ed., *Environmental Biotechnology*, Vol. 45. Boston: Springer, pp. 307–322.

Weisse, M. & Goldman, E. (2020). We Lost a Football Pitch of Primary Rainforest Every 6 Seconds in 2019. *World Resources Institute*. www.wri.org/blog/2020/06/global-tree-cover-loss-data-2019.

Wersal, L. (1995). Islam and Environmental Ethics: Tradition Responds to Contemporary Challenges. *Zygon*,30(3), 451–459.

Westing, A. H. (1981). Environmental Impact of Nuclear Warfare. *Environmental Conservation*, 8(4), 269–273.

Westing, A. H. (1986). *Global Resources and International Conflict: Environmental Factors in Strategic Policy and Action*. Oxford: Oxford University Press.

Whinfield, E. H. (2001). *Masnavi i Ma'navi: Teachings of Rumi, The Spiritual Couplets of Maulana Jalalu-'d-din Muhammad i Rumi*. Trans. & abridged. Ames: Omphaloskepsis.

White, L. T. (1967). The Historical Roots of Our Ecological Crisis. *Science*, 155(3767), 1203–1207.

WHO & UNICEF. (2021). Progress on Household Drinking Water, Sanitation and Hygiene 2000–2020. www.unicef.org/press-releases/billions-people-will-lack-access-safe-water-sanitation-and-hygiene-2030-unless.

WHO. (2021). New WHO Global Air Quality Guidelines Aim to Save Millions of Lives from Air Pollution. www.who.int/news/item/.

Wirsing, R. G., Stoll, D. C. & Jasparro, C. (2013). *International Conflict over Water Resources in Himalayan Asia*. New York: Palgrave Macmillan.

Yang, T. (2006). Towards an Egalitarian Global Environmental Ethics. In *Environmental Ethics and International Policy*. Paris: UNESCO. http://publishing.unesco.org/chapter/978-2-3-104039-0.pdf.

Yūsuf, A. (1979). *Kitāb al-Kharāj*. Cairo: Maktabah al-Qāhirah

Zaidi, I. H. (1981). On the Ethics of Man's Interaction with the Environment: An Islamic Approach. *Environmental Ethics*, 3(1), 35–47.

Zaman, S. M. (1986). Place of Man in the Universe in the World – View of Islam. *Islamic Studies*, 25(3), 325–331.

Zaroug, A. H. (1999). Ethics from an Islamic Perspective: Basic Issues. *American Journal of Islamic Social Sciences*, 16(3), 45–64.

Cambridge Elements

Islam and the Sciences

Nidhal Guessoum

American University of Sharjah, United Arab Emirates

Nidhal Guessoum is Professor of Astrophysics at the American University of Sharjah, United Arab Emirates. Besides Astrophysics, he has made notable contributions in Science & Islam/ Religion, education, and the public understanding of science; he has published books on these subjects in several languages, including *The Story of the Universe* (in Arabic, first edition in 1997), *Islam's Quantum Question* (in English in 2010, translated into several languages), and *The Young Muslim's Guide to Modern Science* (in English 2019, translated into several languages), numerous articles (academic and general-public), and vast social-media activity.

Stefano Bigliardi

Al Akhawayn University in Ifrane, Morocco

Stefano Bigliardi is Associate Professor of Philosophy at Al Akhawayn University in Ifrane, Morocco. He trained as a philosopher of science, has a PhD in philosophy from the University of Bologna, and has been serving in different positions at universities in Germany, Sweden, Mexico, and Switzerland. He has published a monograph and a general-public book on Islam and Science as well as dozens of articles (peer-reviewed and popular) on the subject and others. Since 2016, he has taught undergraduate courses on Islam and Science at Al Akhawayn University in Ifrane, Morocco.

About the Series

Elements in Islam and the Sciences is a new platform for the exploration, critical review and concise analysis of Islamic engagements with the sciences: past, present and future. The series will not only assess ideas, arguments and positions; it will also present novel views that push forward the frontiers of the field. These Elements will evince strong philosophical, theological, historical, and social dimensions as they address interactions between Islam and a wide range of scientific subjects.

Cambridge Elements

Islam and the Sciences

Elements in the Series

Islam and Science: Past, Present, and Future Debates
Nidhal Guessoum and Stefano Bigliardi

Islam's Encounter with Modern Science: A Mismatch Made in Heaven
Taner Edis

Islam and Environmental Ethics
Muhammad Yaseen Gada

A full series listing is available at: www.cambridge.org/EISC